Benjamin Ward Richardson

The Son of a Star

A Romance of the Second Century Vol. 2

Benjamin Ward Richardson

The Son of a Star
A Romance of the Second Century Vol. 2

ISBN/EAN: 9783744776424

Printed in Europe, USA, Canada, Australia, Japan

Cover: Foto ©Thomas Meinert / pixelio.de

More available books at **www.hansebooks.com**

THE
SON OF A STAR

A ROMANCE OF THE SECOND CENTURY

BY

BENJAMIN WARD RICHARDSON

IN THREE VOLUMES

VOL. II.

'*Ficta voluptatis causâ sit proxima veris*'—Hor.

LONDON
LONGMANS, GREEN, AND CO.
AND NEW YORK: 15 EAST 16th STREET
1888

All rights reserved

CONTENTS

OF

THE SECOND VOLUME.

CHAPTER		PAGE
I.	THE LAST ENEMY	1
II.	ASHES TO ASHES	6
III.	IMPERIAL TASKS	28
IV.	A MARCH THROUGH BRITAIN	49
V.	THE NOVIOMAGIANS	66
VI.	LOVE AND LEVIATHAN	97
VII.	ANTINOUS AND FAME	122
VIII.	LATENT WAR	140
IX.	IN LIGHT AND IN SHADOW	170
X.	ROMAN AND JEW	181
XI.	AN AMBASSADOR FROM CÆSAR	195
XII.	THE MISSION TO ITS CLOSE	215
XIII.	ANTINOUS NO MORE	228
XIV.	BETROTHED TO FATE	259
XV.	TO BITHER, 'THE HOUSE OF LIBERTY'	278

THE SON OF A STAR.

CHAPTER I.

THE LAST ENEMY.

EXCEPT the sentinels, the soldiers of the Roman encampment are all in their tents as the escort which bears the relics from the great fire enters the eastern gate. Here, acting under orders, the members of the escort proceed at a slow and quiet pace to their own quarters. dismount with equal quietude, litter down their steeds, pile their arms, and leaving the trophies they have carried in the possession of their leader, straightway seek their own tents.

Severus remains a log, and Tinnius Rufus disturbs his companions by laughing at him in his sleep.

Fidelis the centurion, one hundred years and one day old, lies in the arms of death, and Huldah sits by his couch.

Tryphon the physician has prepared her for what is to come, has foreshadowed the hour of the great struggle: has told her that when the candle that marks the night has burned down three lines more the hour is at hand.

The first line has already burned away.

She is murmuring in gentle voice one of the songs of her childhood and, as if adapting it to the fate of a Roman about to depart, sings it in the Latin tongue:—

> 'Great travail is there for man,
> A heavy yoke on sons of men;
> From the womb of their mother
> Back to the mother of all.
> They think of things to come,
> And of the day of death;
> From him who sitteth on a throne
> To him who is humbled in ashes;
> From him in purple and a crown
> To him in a frock of cloth.
> For the earth must return to the earth
> As the waters return to the sea.'

She ceases on hearing the sound of steps behind her, and a voice, commanding but gentle in tone, breaking in upon her.

'Sing on, sweet watcher, that sweet song; it is a message of truth whoever revealed it.'

She rises, turns to the speaker, and bends low before him. Hadrian! The Cæsar.

'Be seated, child,' adds the Emperor, 'and bend with me to the King who is mightier than I.'

And over the dying soldier, in presence of that mightier king, the ruler of the Empire with head uncovered bends, with the Jewish maiden, to the unseen conqueror of life.

Bringing her lips near to the ear of the dying centurion she whispers the one word: 'Cæsar.'

The effect of the word is magical over the prostrate man at the gate of death.

By an effort unexpected and seemingly supernatural he rises from his couch, glances eagerly at the laurel chaplet that has a few hours before encircled his brow, as if to see that it is safe by his side, seizes his spear at his right hand, raises himself to his feet, and stands erect, like a true soldier, before the Commander of all the Legions.

The last act of reverence and duty.

The last act of a brave soldier.

It is the truest, highest homage that ever Hadrian has received. Incense has been burnt to him as to a god; men have fallen at his feet; but this is the incense of the heart, the homage of the most faithful in its fullest acceptation.

It is but a momentary homage, the dying flicker of soldierly duty; for were it not for Hadrian's and Huldah's help Fidelis had fallen to the earth. They lay him once more on his couch, and soon, breathing more freely, he shows signs of returning power. Another flicker of the expiring flame.

He makes no second attempt to rise, but with feeble gesture requests Huldah to retire that he and Hadrian may be left alone.

The conference between these two remarkable representatives of Roman rule and power is so prolonged that before it ceases the candle burns nearly to the line of fate.

What transpires in that conference need not now be told, but it may be related that from the same hour the conduct of Hadrian towards Huldah, the maiden of Israel, undergoes a change which shapes his destiny and hers.

A call from Hadrian brings the maiden

back to the side of the centurion. The time has truly come ; the candle is burning to the death line, and Fidelis is bearing it company.

The hand of the centurion of one hundred years and one day is grasped in the hand of the Emperor of the World.

Huldah smooths the pillow of the couch, and Emperor and maiden, each with tearful eyes, watch for the end.

'What, child, are the words he is saying? Bend down thine ear, and listen and tell me.'

· Fidelis of Cæsarea.'

The watchword of the night.

The candle burns to the appointed line, and now at the back of the Emperor appears Tryphon the physician.

' Fidelis of Cæsarea!' once more murmurs the sinking man, but so inaudibly that the movement of his lips rather than the sounds produced give the watchword.

The watchword of the night.

The candle burns below the line and holds its own. The Emperor, the physician, the maiden burn on, and hold their own.

Fidelis of one hundred years and one day holds his own no more.

CHAPTER II.

ASHES TO ASHES.

It is one of the chief characteristics of the illustrious man who at this time rules over the Empire of Rome, for him to enter with an ardour almost approaching to fanaticism into any and every cause he has espoused. It is said of him that he is made up of causes.

Let the Emperor take up a thing, and the thing is done: let him take up a person, and that person is made. By these extremes of action he is wearing out his peace of mind; is wearying of the world at one moment, is finding some new and absorbing diversion the next which fills him for a time and leaves him emptier than ever. Three things save him from complete collapse, his strength of will, his versatility, and the perfect simplicity of his life.

By this period, although he has been but a

short time the wearer of the imperial purple, he is almost tired of the cares of it. To rest at Rome in dignity and splendour were quite impossible. Neither his restlessness nor his simplicity of living could bear that strain. He is, therefore, always on the travel; he is determined to see every thing and every people under the sway of his sceptre. If the senate at the centre of the empire presumes to dispute his ruling he will soon be back with them and will measure their power. The senate is closeted with luxury, he is out with the army, but so well organised is the army through all its parts, that he is in continuous touch with Rome. A living chain of communication extends from him to every part of his dominions.

The versatility of his movements is the reflex of the versatility of his nature. He knows something of everything, and he discusses with everybody, however simple, however learned, that which each one knows best. If he is wrong he still discusses, and woe be to the man who corrects him. Favorinus, a mathematician, disputes with him on a mechanical problem, and leaves him as if he were the victor. Why, ask the friends of the philosopher, did you give way to the man when you were so easily shown to be right? How, asks the mathematician in return, how can I be right before that ruler of thirty legions, who killed Appolodorus, the architect, for criticising a fort which he, the ruler, had devised?

To these traits of mastery over men and fortune Hadrian adds others which greatly influence his career. He is touched to the very heart with superstitious sentiments, and at this moment is more than usually under their spell. In his early career he visited the Syrian temple of Apollo near Antioch, from whence flowed the Castalian stream. Into that stream he dropped a leaf of an immortal plant, and from the signs left on the leaf read, through a priestess of the magnificent pile, his life to come. Hitherto that prophetic reading has, in some mysterious manner, been correctly carried out; at least he thinks it has, which is quite sufficient, and now a new sentence of it is, to his mind, being faithfully unfolded.

He had read that he would one day meet

a maiden of divine power who should be deeply learned in religious mysteries, who should perform miraculous deeds, who should be recognised and named for what she could do, who, preserved in purity by his will, should save him from great danger, who should die for his safety and sake, and living again for his fame should carry his name with hers to all posterity.

Whenever she appears let him, Hadrian, take her under his solemn protection, save her from all risk as a priestess of a divine mission, put her in any disguise to keep her from evil, and never more leave him whose life she shall, in recompense, preserve from peril of violent death.

It is a supreme moment with Hadrian. Death he fears not, nay, he sometimes yearns for it, if it would come softly and like a shadow; but a violent death that he shrinks from fearfully. Trajan, a soldier, courted such a death; Hadrian, a philosopher, dare not even contemplate it.

It is a supreme moment: the prophecy is once more being fulfilled: the predicted maiden is found: some even call her divine;

with his own eyes he has seen her perform one of the supremest miracles known to man. She has cast out an evil spirit. It may be she could raise the dead!

Huldah, clad in robes of mourning, stands before him in his own tent, to which she has been summoned. He accosts her by her name, the name of the prophetess after whom she is called.

'Tell me, Huldah, canst thou cast out all evil spirits?'

'Yea, my lord, when the evil spirit doth declare itself to men.'

'Canst thou read mysteries?'

'Yea, my lord, many mysteries!'

'Canst thou forecast events?'

'Yea, my lord.'

'Couldst thou raise the dead centurion to life?'

'Yea, my lord, I did so, that my lord might speak with him, but he wished it not again, so his spirit is now far away in the regions where there is no darkness, and his body is laid ready for the pyre.'

'Thy words are wise. The ashes of Fidelis

alone shall remain on the earth with a stone for his name.'

The smile of triumph which lighted up her face is followed by a look not of fear, that were impossible, but of supplication.

He reads it as such, and asks with subdued eagerness :—

'Maiden, can I serve thee?'

'You can even save me,' was the firm reply.

'From what or whom?'

'Severus.'

'By all the Cæsars, I interpreted him aright,' thought Hadrian, as he recalled the incidents of the previous day.

Then, turning to her, he made with her an imperial contract, closer, holier than any he had made before with any king or potentate whatsoever.

'Trust me, maiden; obey what I shall command, however strange it be to thee, and thou art safe as the holiest virgin of the most sacred Temple.

'In return thou must abide ever near to me, and guide me in mine hours of need by thy foreknowledge and wisdom.

'And, if I bid thee change thy name and semblance of thy sex thou must obey.'

'I am at my lord's command.'

Huldah is returning from the imperial tent as Severus enters. He hears her receive the imperial permission that Fidelis shall have public funeral rites, and so soon as he is alone with his master he takes charge of the promise as an imperial order, and goes forth to see it executed. So in a few short hours it happens that the camp, which was a scene of such wild festivity, is transformed into a scene of mourning and sorrow.

A spear turned point downwards into the earth, and carrying a small dark banner, a mere strip, but sufficient when many times repeated to cause a saddening gloom, is at the door of every tent. But the gloom of glooms is the silence; the musical instruments are all silent, the new watchword of the sentinels '*In pace*,' is said in a whisper, and out of his quarters no man speaks a word. The men who, in the great arena, prepare the pyre communicate to each other by signs, their voices are still.

The gallants of the night before, in their fretfulness, keep to their couches and console themselves with wine. Milo of the menagerie keeps the wolves and other wild beasts quiet by plying them well with food.

Fabius and Vibullius remain in their quarters, and amuse themselves by old stories in which Severus and the Emperor play a leading part.

Saserna composes a dismal dirge.

Rufus with quiet delight visits his virago, to enjoy the sight of seeing her afraid to open her mouth, and is so pleased with the effect that for the first time for many months he gives her a warm caress, to the virago's wonder, and, to speak honestly, happiness.

Severus returns to his home in the pine wood, and nourishing a thousand jealousies of Cæsar, and planning battles to come, studies maps and plans, arranges trophies, and drinks wine.

The Emperor is closeted with Tryphon his trusted physician and friend, and as their consultation affects this history deeply, let us listen to them a moment as they converse.

The Emperor has told his friend the story

of the prophecy of the priestess of the temple near to Antioch, and Tryphon readily feeds the conviction his master entertains, while like a philosopher he himself scorns the superstition attached to it.

'I knew that priestess,' says he, 'she was very wise, she read the very hearts of men; once she was beautiful, as beautiful as any of my race, to which she belonged; so beautiful that Trajan himself almost died for her love. Had his Empress, the revengeful Plotina, known of her, I fear me, Prince, that all her charms, divine and human, had not saved her.'

For some moments the Emperor thought intensely over these words. They were a new light to him; then he broke the silence by a passing observation.

'His love, my Tryphon, had been thrown away on the priestess of Daphne.'

'Nay! nay! nay! if so I may speak. That woman loved Trajan even to madness, even to death.'

Once more the Emperor was deep in thought. At length he rose, and pushing away the papers and books which lay before him he turned to another topic.

'Tryphon, I want thy aid.'

'The will of Cæsar rules his servant.'

'It is a service delicate and requiring all thy skill.'

'Whatever skill I have is thine.'

'The dead man, Tryphon, the centurion Fidelis of a hundred years for a few moments rose from death at the command of that maiden whom they call Huldah, in order to leave her in sacred charge to my care, and, mark the words, to my care for my own safety.'

'And you accepted the charge?'

'With all the heart of Cæsar.'

'It is well, the woman is wise. She is learned in all the knowledge of Egypt and all the books of our father Israel. What wouldest thou of the maiden?'

'Let the prophecy concerning her be fulfilled. Let her remain ever by my side.'

''Twere dangerous, Prince, in whatever innocence it were done. The Empress would never forgive.'

'I know it too well, but there is even a greater danger.'

'Thou meanest in Julius Severus.'

'I do. He loves the maiden with such madness that he would make her his lawful wife and do anything she might demand; failing in that he would place her with the dead rather than see her amongst the living as another one's belonging.'

'The words of Cæsar are most true.'

'Therefore I want thy skill. Transform the maiden into a youth who may without suspicion attend on me.'

'You ask a miracle.'

'Nay, my good Tryphon, if I asked for a miracle, to her, not to thee, should I apply; to thee I turn for earthly miracles, which thou canst perform so well.'

'Let my lord point the way.'

'In Bithynia thou broughtest to me from thy friend Pliny a youth, the very second self of this maiden, the youth we call Antinous. During this coming funereal rite let Huldah assume the dress of this youth, his name, and afterwards his office as cup-bearer to me. For Antinous himself find a mission far away; let him have means and, under a new name, the chance to win a soldier's fortune. Of ambition he has more than enough; of reticence the firmness of a diamond. A single letter will change his name; bid him in his new career be Antoninus and all will go well. He has the genius for disguise from a slave to an emperor.'

'And Huldah, my lord?'

'Let it appear that she has fled after the Jew who ran as the living torch.'

'But his remains are found; 'twere vain for her to follow him.'

'Nay, there thou trippest, Tryphon; a woman thinks nothing vain in love. The madder the act the more likely is the act to be accredited. Moreover, she may not have known of the remains when she fled away.'

'Cæsar were a soothsayer were he not Cæsar. It shall all be done. To-night Huldah, the maiden of Cæsarea, for 'twas there she was born, shall be Antinous the favourite cup-bearer of the emperor of all the world.'

These designs for the change in her career have been made, and Huldah sits by the side of the dead Fidelis, waiting for the decline of the sun and the lighting of the pyre. Strange and even to herself inscrutable are her own thoughts. She has conversed with Hadrian as she had never conversed before with any one. She has been visited by the learned Tryphon, has heard from him the part she is to play, and has freely consented to the proposition.

She has pledged herself to obedience to the will of Cæsar in all honour. He is a man and a prince, and yet she trusts him. She will do his will and serve him, and if the prophecy be true she will save him from a violent death. Then her services to him are fulfilled, and Simeon and her people are her future masters.

She has heard of the return of the search party, and although the finding has not been publicly proclaimed she has been told of it. It affects her no wise anxiously, for she is firm in her faith that no mortal hand can kill Simeon, her beloved and only absolute lord.

Yet while she believes with all her heart, her reason is on the outlook; she listens as if she were waiting for tidings that shall confirm her beliefs.

The tidings come.

Eli the faithful enters the tent, kneels reverently with head uncovered to the corpse of Fidelis, and then still kneeling bends to his divine mistress.

Oh happy mistress of one so truly faithful!

She gives him her hand to rise and feels the thrill, the unconscious thrill that crosses it. He seats himself before her, as to her, with palpitating heart, he tells his adventure.

He has obeyed her commands to the letter. He has followed Simeon, has seen his rescue, has seen the Roman soldiers befooled, and has left him travelling westward with his deliverers and guides, happy as he is safe with them, and as if he were their own!

Quiet, palpitating heart; no, not so suddenly quiet, or thou wilt, for a moment, stop and betray thy secret to him who of all others must not guess it.

The mind conquers as Huldah with studied serenity thanks her friend; then she confides to him her new destiny and asks him if, for a season, freedman as he is, he will serve her still.

It is a foregone conclusion that he should assent. What shall be his next service?

'Follow, faithful Eli, follow those fugitives,

and from them, from time to time, come to me. Wherever Hadrian shall be there am I, as Antinous his favourite cup-bearer. From the moment when the fire leaps up over the body of yon dead man Huldah will have left the camp, as all shall believe save Hadrian, his physician, Tryphon, thou and I. 'Twill be easy at all times to find the resting place of Cæsar.'

He kneels once more as she extends her hand, kisses it with trembling lips, and in a moment is gone on his further mission, the truest messenger of love and duty that earth, in most heavenly mood, ever gave forth to man or woman born.

Maiden, still clad in thine own attire, rise from thy seat of mourning, put on thy new attire, and transform thyself into a man.

Truly thou art a cup-bearer worthy of Cæsar!

The sun is going down, and there is some gentle noise in the camp as of men solemnly and silently gathering in array. Over that boy's attire cast thy woman's habit of mourning, shroud thy temples and place thyself at the head of Fidelis, for the bier and the bearers come with muffled step and voiceless lips to carry him forth.

On the breast of the old centurion rests his laurel crown, and by his side the long-used sword, the vitis, the spear. His armour is on him as if he were going forth to fight another foe.

Huldah, as chief mourner, precedes the bier.

Outside the tent the bearers rest a moment for all to form in order.

At the foot of the bier, habited as a plain soldier, is Hadrian with his head uncovered. Behind him the white-robed priests; behind them Severus, and behind him all the chiefs of the Imperial and vice-Imperial household. Only two march out of the rank, Saserna as master of the ceremonial and his marshal or trumpeter.

The troops line the way on each side in double column from the encampment into the arena, the place of the pyre. Their spears are turned point downwards to the earth, and their uncovered heads are bent in reverence to the dead.

'Why,' asks Fabian of the ruddy Tinnius, 'why do not the priests chant and pour forth the incense to Pluto and the infernal gods?'

'Because,' answers Rufus, who even in this solemn moment can hardly suppress a smile, 'because the infernal gods have told Cæsar they don't wish it, and Cæsar has told the priests, and Fidelis has left no money for their pious frauds. Huldah is the high priestess this time. Listen to her voice.'

As they march on, the troops falling in and following in order, she chants in low voice a plaint of a Chaldean song:—

'Man that is born of a woman
Is of few days and full of trouble.

He cometh forth as a flower and is cut down,
He fleeth as a shadow and continueth not.

Man dieth and wasteth away,
Yea, he giveth up the spirit, and where is he?

As the waters fail from the sea
And the flood decayeth and drieth up,

So man lieth down and riseth not
Till the heavens be no more.

They shall not awake
Nor be raised out of their sleep.'

The song continues until the cortège reaches the arena. Reverently and gently the dead body of Fidelis with all that belongs to it, is laid on the pyre.

The soldiers form around the pyre in a semi-circle, with the Emperor, Severus, and their officers in the centre. Huldah moves round to the opposite side of the pyre, where she stands majestically alone.

The sun has fallen, the light of day is sinking into gloom, and heavy clouds of darkness hang like curtains of mourning around, yet spitting forth their tongues of lightning and of portending storm.

Saserna gives a sign; the trumpet peals forth; a youth belonging to the train of the Emperor bears to him, the central figure of the group, an unlighted torch. Then he gives a lighted torch to Severus, who with it lights that which has been handed to Cæsar.

A second, a third blast from the trumpet and Cæsar with his own hand sets the pyre aflame.

The furze that forms the basis of the pyre begins to crackle and blaze, the clouds of mourning grow denser, and distant thunder rolls ; the fire and smoke begin to ascend. Huldah stands alone, as if she would leap into the flames from the raised mound on which her feet rest.

Suddenly she breaks forth into loud song, before which the white-robed priests behind Hadrian bend in awe, it is so weird and wonderful :—

> ' His eyes are the eyelids of the morning,
> Out of his mouth go burning lamps,
> And sparks of fire leap out.
>
> Out of his nostrils goeth smoke,
> And a flame goeth out of his mouth.
>
> The arrow cannot make him flee,
> Sling stones are with him as stubble;
> Darts are counted as stubble,
> He laugheth at the shaking of a spear.
>
> He maketh a path to shine after him,
> A king above all the children of pride.
>
> Where is the way where light dwelleth ? '

As she repeats this last line with increasing richness and fulness of voice, the pyre rises into such vivid blaze and brightness that they around it retire backwards from it, and the lonely singer is hidden by it from their view. Yet still her voice is heard, as again with stronger emphasis it asks of the consuming dead:

'Where is the way where light dwelleth?

The fire begins to fade, and the Emperor prepares to leave. At the trumpet-call a centurion proceeds to tell out his hundred men to surround and watch out the fire, and gather the ashes of him of a hundred years. The handsome youth who brought the torch has been to the tent to fetch a cloak for Hadrian, for the air is becoming cold. The youth returns, and with grace and dignity places the cloak on the shoulders of Cæsar; and, followed by the rest, marches with him back to the encampment.

It is Hadrian's hour for repose, and receiving the salutations of Severus and the officers at the door of his pavilion he retires from the scene.

Severus retires also to his quarters, but not to rest. Much wine lashes him into a demon. He paces the floors of his house alone, impatient of news that is to come.

The footsteps of a guard at last break his fury, and the captain of the guard stands before him pale and tremulous.

'The woman is what I want before me, not thou alone; why keepest thou her back an instant?'

'My lord——'

'The woman, I tell thee; let me see that thou hast her safe?'

'My lord, she is not——'

'What sayest thou, miscreant?' screams the furious Severus, as he lays his hand on his sword. 'If thou sayest she has escaped I will smite thee to the earth.'

'My breast is open to thee,' rejoins the soldier, now no longer in fear; 'let Severus smite to death his faithful Varus, but the truth must be told: the Jewish maiden, Huldah, is not in the encampment.'

Returning his sword to his side, Severus gasps the words, 'Go on, tell everything.'

'The Jewish maiden Huldah disappeared as her voice died away before the pyre of Fidelis; 'tis thought she leaped into the flames and died by his side.

'Let not a scruple of the ashes of that fire be left unturned in search for any fragment of her that may remain. Away! in every quarter double the watches, and, until the broad day, permit not one person, not Cæsar himself, to leave the camp. He is only a soldier, and none need know him as Cæsar.'

The officer, the most trusted of all who worshipped Julius Severus, and he had his worshippers, as all great men have, hastened to his duty, leaving his master once more to himself and his master's master, wine.

'Fool that I am, befooled! befooled! But for thee I were Cæsar, and Hadrian nowhere. I'll touch thee never more, thou flagoned thief! I'll cast thee forth from the pure vase that holds thee as that woman I worship casts out demons. She, and she alone, would save me from thy fiendship. But she is not, and thou art! Thy breath is sweet, thy colour entrancing, thy taste precious. One final love.

In his haste, the flagoned thief is raised to his conquered lips without being measured forth even in the goblet. And Severus the soldier is once more Severus the log.

CHAPTER III.

IMPERIAL TASKS.

THE journey which Hadrian is now making through the remote island of Britain gives rise to many a flying and an unexpected visit. A few years previously, three years after he mounted the throne on the death of Trajan, Hadrian had travelled through the island on a tour which he rendered historical by commencing during it the construction of a wall destined to extend from Tunnocelum to Segedunum, a line of seventy-four Roman miles, for protecting the Britannic part of the island from the Mæatæ who invaded it constantly from the north.

Anxious to see how this great work is progressing, Hadrian, being in Gaul, comes over to Britain with a small guard, and in such haste that he carries with him little more than the common soldier's garb in which he usually travels. He enjoys the journey. To fall in upon his generals and see the encampments suddenly and without notice or ceremonial is the very thing that suits his versatile humour. He has now dropt on Julius Severus, a man for whose military skill he has the profoundest admiration, and for whom, in all else, he has the most utter contempt, amounting to personal dislike. It delights him therefore that he has outwitted Severus in strategy, has found out his deepest secret, and has stolen, literally, his heart.

The Emperor, according to his custom, rises with the sun, and workmen are speedily closeted with him taking an order from his own lips and hand. The ashes of Fidelis are to be placed in an urn, and over the urn there is to be set a block of stone. On one side of the stone there is to be carved a bold relief of the centurion four feet high and that will last for ages. It is to show the man in his power, with his armour, sword and vitis, and below is to be inscribed word for word what he the Cæsar indites, signed with the dipla > or triangle without a base, the symbol of a centurion.

TADIA VALLAUNIUS T. V. POL.
FIDELIS > LEG. II. AUG.
HADRIANUS IMP. POSUIT.
II. S. E.
VIXIT ANNIS CENTUM.

It tells in that Tadia Vallaunius, son of Tadia Vallaunius of the tribe Pollia, was a centurion called Fidelis of the second Augustan Legion; that the monument was erected by the Emperor Hadrian; that the ashes of Fidelis rest under the monument (*Hic Situs Est*); and that he was a hundred years old.

This arranged, the order goes forth that all the encampment is to pass before Cæsar in review, with Severus in command.

Tinnius Rufus bears the order to Severus.

Saserna, the Editor of Ceremonies, receives the next instruction, namely, that after the review the Emperor will sup with Severus and the chief officers, and on the following morning at sunrise will depart with his retinue towards the north to the great wall.

The drowsy Severus receives the Imperial message with wooden stolidity; but Rufus knows his man, and leads him slowly and surely into action. A prayer is sent to the Emperor that the review may be delayed until noon, and the prayer is readily granted.

Cæsar with his suite will ride into the country, while Severus puts the troops into order.

Cæsar rides forth, Antinous by his side mounted on a charger somewhat smaller but as spirited as the charger which he himself bestrides.

'By Jupiter, how grandly the new Antinous sits in the saddle! Such skill, such art, such mastery! It must be the first hour for putting forth such accomplishment, but the skill is matchless.'

Tryphon, also mounted and near the Emperor, sees the effect, and shares in the admiration.

'Tryphon, this Antinous is truly divine; 'tis blasphemy to change that title.'

'Nay, Prince, the title is not materially changed as to its meaning; the term Antinous by its native original sense means "before of us;" it now revives its first intention.'

'Fate, like water, finds its own level, my Tryphon. But tell me something of these miraculous gifts. I have read that when Vespasian was in Alexandria they brought to him a blind and a lame man; that he anointed the eyes of the blind man with spittle and lifted the hand of the lame man; whereupon the blind man was at once enabled to see and the lame man to walk. Thinkest thou that to be true?'

'Tis well vouched for by those who were present.'

'Thinkest thou that these powers, which our new Antinous owns, could be transferred to me?'

'In the presence of Antinous they might, but not otherwise.'

'Would that we could try them.'

''Tis easily done. In a village near lives a worker in clay, a native prince of great skill and fame. He hath lost the use of his hands, and my fame having gone round as thy physician, his friends have sought my aid in vain. I would gladly be outdone by Cæsar should they call for his interposition.'

It is the will of Cæsar to visit the house of the worker in clay straightway.

For the remainder of the journey, Antinous

and Tryphon ride side by side. They converse in their native Hebrew tongue. They seem to have some dispute, in which Tryphon laughs at his comrade's sturdy belief and self-confidence, but in the end appears to accept, with reservation, what is told to him; and so, understanding each other, they reach their destination.

Segonax the potter, descendant of one who had fought against the first Cæsar, is sitting in his workshop, his glorious works of art in clay surrounding him, as this latest of Cæsars enters. His hands droop helplessly by his side: the wheel and the clay are before him, and his feet can work the wheel, but his hands cannot touch or work the clay.

The wife of Segonax hears who visits them, and soon she and the other women ask, 'Cannot Cæsar cure a palsied man?'

'If thou shouldst fail, great king, the blame be with us. But try thy power, it may be great.'

Antinous stands beside the Cæsar, wrapt in trance, holding his left hand. Hadrian hesitates; then, with his own right hand he takes up first the right, next the left, hand of Segonax and bids him resume his labour.

It is the work of a moment; Segonax believes and his faith heals him. He clutches the clay, and, to the Emperor's proud delight, a vase of exquisite form is being shaped for him by the hands he has restored to activity and skill.

No, not hands restored by him, but by Antinous the divine, the 'before all of us.'

'Let the vase be cast in gold. Let Segonax be a freed man of Rome.'

'Let Segonax as a native prince show his gratitude by coming to Rome as the guest of Cæsar.'

It shall all be as Cæsar wills.

Back to the camp in triumph, where, ere the review commences, it is related far and wide, with awe and wonder, that Cæsar has restored, by a miracle, the dead hands of Segonax the potter.

THE REVIEW.

Into the vast plain below the camp, Severus at their head, the whole encampment marches. Severus rides like the wind in massing his troops, so that from the stand where Hadrian is placed all may be seen in grand array. Hadrian, nobly mounted, rides well, but not like Severus. The pride of Severus must be taken down.

Antinous, in the dress of a Roman soldier, rides modestly in the rear of the Imperial staff.

Cæsar calls for Antinous.

'Thou art my messenger. Swift as Mercury convey this message to Severus, and back to my side.'

Magnificent! Bearing the flag of Cæsar's messenger Antinous flies through files and squadrons: rides as if the horse and the rider were one; the troops can scarcely restrain their enthusiasm, and a suppressed cheer does not escape the ear of the general as the strange messenger, doffing cap and dropping flag, puts the message into his hands.

It is a complimentary message, that the order of the troops is splendid and worthy of Julius Severus.

Sweet flattery carried on a poisoned dart. For as the messenger returns, bowing to the troops and flying without so much as touching the rein, they almost recognise Mercury in human form.

Even Severus cannot ride like that, is what the whole camp feels, and Severus knows it. Never before was such a thing seen. Cæsar also comments on the riding of Severus in words which will reach him too soon.

'Next to Antinous, Severus is the best horseman I have ever seen.'

The troops defile before the Prince of men as if indeed he were more than mortal, Severus on one side of him, Antinous on the other. It has long been known that the young Antinous is a favourite of favourites, but never before has such attention been shown him. Is it the skill of horsemanship that has so captivated the master of the legions?

Antinous is from Bithynia, and 'all Bithynians are born on a horse,' is the proverb which goes from mouth to mouth.

The troops return to the camp, are bidden to regale at the expense of the Emperor, and within an hour are hastening to the Prætorium to listen to or read the Proclamation which he has sent forth.

A PROCLAMATION.

THE SALUTATION OF HADRIAN TO THE SOLDIERS OF TH LEGIONS WHICH HAVE PASSED BEFORE HIM THIS DAY.

The discipline, the skill in the use of arms, the marching order, the firmness, the intelligence, reflect the supremest credit on all concerned, from the illustrious general, Julius Severus, to the youngest soldier in the ranks, and implant the firmest confidence in the heart of Cæsar.

The same shall be conveyed, by special messenger, to the Senate and to Rome.

Julius Severus is raised to the rank of Governor-General of all Britain.

Tinnius Rufus is promoted to the personal Staff of Cæsar.

Segonax, the potter, is made a freed man of Rome, and has restored to him his native princely title for the great skill he has shown in his ancient art.

Antinous, faithful attendant of Cæsar, is made a knight of the Roman Empire.

AVE CÆSAR!

Ave Cæsar! is the song of the camp as Saserna concludes the pronouncement of this proclamation, and young Antinous is the idol of the hour.

The four gallants, who had been so cruelly cheated out of the Numidian bear, declare they must have Antinous amongst them, and seek an introduction.

Fabius, Vibullius, Saserna and Rufus, in the quarters of Rufus, hold a symposium preparatory to the great banquet which is to bid farewell to an Emperor and to introduce a Governor of all Britain.

They congratulate Rufus as a matter of course; they banter him also to their hearts' content. Fabius suggests, with becoming gravity, that Cæsar has caught a great satirical poet, and means to crown the illustrious rival of Juvenal with the laurel, on return to Rome.

Vibullius believes that Cæsar has been seduced by the virago Boadicea, and suggests that Rufus will soon be disposed of as Governor of some remote colony where wives are not allowed to follow. Saserna, on the other hand, argues that this elevation of Rufus is a cleverly devised plot arranged through Severus, by which he, Rufus, may get away from Boadicea and leave her in her native country to do as best she can.

Let him laugh who wins; nothing that is said can upset the good nature of the jovial Red-beard. That he will have some trouble with Boadicea he knows, for she is a woman as difficult to take away as to leave behind. But then he has Cæsar at his back ; Cæsar's word is stronger than Boadicea's, and he, therefore, cannot be blamed for a fate that must be.

Tired of teasing their comrade or finding that they fail to tease, they turn their tongues next on the rising sun of Antinous.

Saserna, supposed to know everything, is called on to tell them who this Antinous is.

Saserna knows no more than that the favourite came in the train of the Emperor ; is said to have been born of humble parentage in Bithynia ; was sent by Pliny the younger, when he was pro-consul of Bithynia, to Hadrian, in the first year of his reign, as a boy who had shown great capacity for natural knowledge ; and that Hadrian, taking a liking to him, retained him, but never until this day showed him such marks of favour.

'It is one of the fits of Cæsar,' observes Vibullius, ' to take these astounding fancies. You or I, my Fabius, might live in his sight for ever and never receive a mark of favour, but let an Antinous—— '

'Or a Tinnius,' interposed Fabius.

' Or a Tinnius ; yes, or a Tinnius,' resumed

Vibullius, 'appear, and up he goes, like a stone from a catapult.'

'To rise truly,' broke in Saserna, 'and as certainly to fall. Thanks to the gods, including Hadrian, I have neither to rise nor fall.'

'It is not from want of making yourself heard, Saserna, at all events,' puts in the rosy host with excellent humour. 'And now,' he adds, 'if your jealousies are quite appeased let me remind you that the banquet time is at hand and that we must attire for it.'

A FEAST.

It is a noble feast served in the banqueting room of the Prætorium; for Severus, with the help of Tinnius and Saserna, can plan a feast as ably as a siege.

To Hadrian the whole ceremony is a pain. It is a true pleasure to him to sup with a few congenial souls, throw off the imperial purple, argue, laugh, sing, and joke; but ceremonial, he is weary of it as he is weary almost of the world.

Much pleasure hath made him sad, so he declares every day of his life. It is the open secret of his restlessness, that he must move and work in order to live with a clear and active mind, and without despair.

In a pavilion at the back of the seat of state placed for the Emperor the various officers of the encampment are brought to him for introduction, to all of whom he speaks kindly and freely. But his mind is gloomy. The awful words :—

'Remember thou art but a man!'

muttered at fixed intervals, by the standard-bearer behind him, are like the drops of water on the head of the condemned in the torture of the drop-by-drop martyrdom. When will the torture end?

Tryphon at respectful distance reads every line of that sad face, and softly moving round to the standard-bearer whispers him to keep silence. It is done in the most unassuming and quiet manner, but Cæsar observes it, and by a look of gladness conveys his thanks to his wise and honoured physician and friend.

The preliminaries over, every one, except Cæsar, proceeds, in state, to the hall of feasting.

Severus, copying from a native custom, has had the banqueters seated at the tables instead of reclining on couches in Roman fashion.

There are many small tables, each of which receives men of the same rank.

At the head, under a splendid royal canopy, is the single table for Cæsar with a chair of state. On a second table, a little lower down, is the vice-regal place of Severus, to the right of the Emperor.

On the same level, on the left side, is a guest also alone as one of princely dignity.

The Emperor's sole guest, Segonax the Potter!

The gallants standing at their table lower down are stricken blind, deaf, dumb, dead! Segonax, whom they in fun rolled in his own clay but four days agone, and of whom they left a clay effigy with the hands cut off for the helpless creature to stare at in his misery!

He the sole guest of the Emperor! He, seated on a level with Severus the Governor-General of all Britain!

It is well the gallants are bereft of sense at the sight, for did they show any revolt, that same Cæsar who has raised Segonax to greatness will just as easily let them down to a still colder place.

True Emperors are true levellers.

And Hadrian knows it.

Vibullius is startled, but Fabius is filled with admiration. This one act, spread by voice and voice through every native camp of conquered Britain, as a fitting sequel to the miracle, will do more to strengthen the power of Rome in Britain than a hundred battles won by Severus.

'The hearts of men are more easily won than their arms, my Vibullius.'

Tinnius is so delighted he drinks a stoup of wine on the spot. It is a most unmannerly thing to touch either meat or drink until Cæsar sets the example; but Tinnius forgets himself in thinking how easy this act of Cæsar will make his task with Boadicea, who is a relative of the potter.

Severus, in gorgeous toga hemmed with purple, with one profile to the audience and another profile to the throne, stands rigid as marble. He throws a faint smile of recognition towards Segonax as if he were glad of his presence, and in his chilled heart he is as glad as such a heart can let him be; for this friendship with a native chief will make his rule over all Britain as easy as he could wish, and will give him time to plan conquests over better foes than British savages.

The trumpets sound: all knees bend; all heads are bowed low.

The Cæsar enters.

He is still clad in his soldier's garb, but over it is cast the Imperial robe of purple, and round his brow is the light oval of laurel, the crown of the emperors. The sight, so novel to him in every respect, pleases him; he takes up a goblet filled by Antinous, but not with wine.

Saserna speaks for Hadrian.

'Cæsar wishes you all health, happiness and long life, and may the gods command the feast.'

The sound of a clarion very softly uttered tells that the Emperor's pledge is drunken and that he is seated. With one simultaneous '*Ave Cæsar!*' the guests follow his action, and the feast begins.

Like all feasts imperial and unimperial, this feast soon passes away in fumes of wine and noise, leaving the usual emptiness behind it. One incident alone gives to it a peculiarity belonging to our history.

In the course of the banquet, at the proper period, the golden goblet used by the Emperor is removed for a moment, and after its ablution is replaced by his side.

It is charged by his own hands with the wine from which he is supplied. The wine is a thin and acid liquid, but then it is the wine of Cæsar, and who would not relish that? Woe be to him who does not.

Antinous on both bended knees holds the cup while Cæsar charges it, and Saserna declares the imperial will.

'To Severus Governor of all Britain, and to Segonax the Prince and friend of Hadrian.'

Antinous rises, and bearing the cup to Severus, presents it kneeling on his right knee; he then gracefully rises as Severus stands erect, to accept it from his hands. The cup is at the very lips of the Governor of all Britain when the eyes of the Governor meet those of the cup-bearer!

To the consternation of the Emperor and of all the company, except the cup-bearer, the goblet falls from the hands of the Governor of Britain; and the hands fall, as once fell the hands of Segonax.

A worse omen for Julius Severus could not possibly have inaugurated his new reign. Even Cæsar pales.

Antinous turns the scale of fortune back to Severus. Picking up the fallen cup with infinite grace, he uplifts it to show that not a drop of wine is spilled.

Marvellous! Severus may fall but he cannot be injured; the wine of his life cannot flow away. He himself regains his power as the cheers of his audience and the radiant face of Cæsar re-assure him: he retakes the goblet, raises it to his lips, bows to his master, and with averted look returns the cup to the hands that gave it him.

'He might have thought the cup was poisoned,' whispers Fabius to Rufus.

'His gorge rose at the sour drink,' responds the Red beard; 'wine, not vinegar, not even imperial vinegar, for Julius Severus.'

'He has detected us,' says Hadrian, to Hadrian.

'A woman can conceal all her sex except her eyes; and they would betray the wisest of women to the greatest fool of a man,' says Tryphon to Tryphon; 'but this woman has regained her position as Antinous.'

It was as Tryphon thought. The meeting of the eyes of the cup-bearer with the eyes of Severus palsied for the moment the Governor of Britain. No eyes except one pair could transfix like those. Yet 'tis impossible! this cup-bearer came into the camp with Cæsar; has long been known as the favourite Antinous; was sent to Rome from Bithynia by Pliny the consul, and now is kneeling on the left knee to Segonax, presenting to him the goblet as no one who was not trained in a court and to court ceremonial could. Both knees to Cæsar, the right knee to the Governor, the left knee to the Guest; that means years of culture. Then the horsemanship of the morning, no woman could have done that; curse the rider who did!

A bright thought. This cup-bearer this Antinous, by some singular fate is the twin brother of the divine maiden who has gone no one knoweth where.

Drink more wine, Julius Severus; let it confirm thee in this discovery. Bacchus loves to strengthen his worshippers in their own conceits. Thou art a great man, Severus. Bacchus swears it. Thou hast the eye of a hawk, the grip of a leopard, the wisdom of an owl, the courage of a lion, the sweep and swiftness of an eagle. Thou hast, with thy usual powers, solved the mystery. Bacchus swears it. But those eyes, those transfixing eyes. Look at them as they pass thee back to Cæsar; they twinkle with mirth truly, but they are as manly as thine own. See how proudly they fall on Cæsar as the eyes of a foolish page who thinks himself great and who apes nobility.

Thou art right, Severus. Bacchus swears it.

Drink, great Governor of all Britain; drink and confirm thy faith in thine own craftiness! Bacchus is by thy side!

CHAPTER IV.

A MARCH THROUGH BRITAIN.

IN the hour when the sun rises after the banquet to the Cæsar there is commotion in the camp. Cæsar is, as usual, up with the sun and on his day's march, has in truth been up before the sun, and has had his commands executed so quietly and silently that no soldier in the ranks leaving for a ten days' journey could have made less stir.

Severus, after reaching his home from the banquet, has gone soundly into repose. He has previously issued orders that so soon as the sentries see any movement in Hadrian's pavilion he shall be called. He has also given his orders as to the attendants who shall form the escort, and as to the ceremonials which shall be followed when the master of all the legions shall take his departure. Every part of this organisation has been studied with the best skill of the most skilful of Roman generals. It is policy for the Governor of all Britain to show the highest honour to the Governor of all the world. The office of Emperor is not hereditary, and the chances of it are many for Severus. It must be well sustained whoever holds it.

Severus is sound in this calculation, but he is unsound in another calculation : the temper of the man whom he wishes to exalt.

For another edict has gone forth, from Hadrian, and has first obedience.

'Let every person in the train and bodyguard of Cæsar be ready, without any noise of trumpet or call, to march out of the camp during the middle watch, assemble at sunrise outside the northern gate, and there wait for command to proceed into northern Britain.'

The order is obeyed to the letter, and with the first rays of the sun Cæsar himself, accompanied only by Tinnius Rufus, Antinous and Tryphon, their horses preceding them, leave their quarters to join their companions at the place directed.

A dispatch is left for Severus, thanking

that skilful commander for all that he has done, commending the discipline of the camp, and congratulating the Governor of all Britain on his new dignity and extended rule. To Severus Cæsar wishes health and happiness, and farewell.'

The Imperial party reach the northern gate in good time and in quietude. They pass the portal; they find the body-guard all ready to receive the Emperor, and are departing in perfect order, when a rush and a loud scream break the silence and the ceremony.

It is Boadicea, the native wife of Tinnius, accompanied by her relative Segonax the potter, who raises this alarm.

The virago has broken loose from her keeper and from her own word. Tinnius about to escape is once more the prisoner of Boadicea.

Tinnius, foreseeing the storm that would attend his departure, had been, for him, unusually clever. He had made greater friends than ever with Segonax the potter; he had given that native prince a little fortune of Roman coins; he had got Segonax to join in the revelation he had made to Boadicea respecting his attachment to the staff of Cæsar, and he had actually persuaded her, with many tears on her part, to remain with Segonax until his own return.

On this understanding they had a few hours before embraced and kissed their farewells, and now she has returned with the true Boadicean fury upon her in full tide, during which she cares for no man whatsoever.

Segonax does nothing but apologise. Boadicea does nothing but storm and weep. Segonax shows by his clothing what he has gone through, for Boadicea has thrown him into a ditch and torn his clothes, so that he has been obliged to call in the aid of three followers in order to be ready to take her back by force if needs be.

But Boadicea is in no humour to treat with Segonax, neither cares she one straw for Cæsar himself, even if she recognises him amongst the rest of the soldiers, which is not likely.

She looks only for the unhappy Tinnius, into whose arms, to the immense amusement of Hadrian, she throws herself with true feminine vigour and devotion.

To say that she weeps and laments were weak terms indeed. She pours forth torrents of tears and a perfect thunder of words, with lightnings from her red eyes which are alone killing. Segonax tries to drag her away; as well try to tear a limpet from a rock: the more he pulls the more she hugs her Roman spouse.

At last, partly by the efforts of Segonax, and partly by the efforts of Tinnius himself, but mostly by a change of temper in the chief actor in the scene, Boadicea gives way, yet only to create a new movement, which is infinitely more ridiculous.

Seizing the miserable Rufus by his beard with her right hand and Segonax by his neck with her left, she makes a flank movement towards the home of the potter, pushing him and pulling her husband with a rapidity and force that is irresistible.

That she would soon get them both away is more than probable but for the intrepidity of the page Antinous, who, rushing up behind Tinnius, with one stroke of a short sword shaves off the red beard so dexterously that the prisoner is left free to run in an instant back to the body-guard of the Emperor and entrench himself within it, safe for a moment from all peril.

The rage of the virago doubles. Waving the mass of beard, which she still firmly clutches with one hand, she shakes and grasps the unfortunate Segonax with the other so vigorously, that he would surely have been strangled had not a smart blow across the muscles of her arm from the hand of Antinous paralysed her grip and allowed the potter to fall full length upon the earth, black in the face and half-unconscious from the strangulation, but saved in the very nick of time, and protected now by his faithful followers from further molestation. Holding the beard on high like some bloody flag or spoil, Boadicea, shrieking and striking the air, rushes at the whole of the Roman corps, sparing none who dare to speak to her. The Emperor comes in for it worse than any, for thinking him to be no more than a private soldier she rages at his big head and contemptible figure, strikes at him with the beard of Tinnius, and in bad Latin, that she may not be misunderstood, threatens to tear out his eyes. She is quieted once more by Antinous, and after a word with Cæsar and Tryphon, obtained during a moment of respite from the furious tongue, a centurion gives out the order to half a dozen soldiers :—

'Gag the woman's mouth, bind her firmly on the back of a quiet mule, and let her follow with the baggage in the rear under close guard, by request of her husband, and the permission of Cæsar.'

It is all done in a few minutes without further noise. The Boadicean storm is over, the soldiers are skilful and strong, the mule is ready, and the virago is as dumb and obedient as the animal which carries her. Her arms are bound down to her sides, with just sufficient freedom to her hands to enable her to hold the reins : the beard of Tinnius is tied to the mane of the mule as a kind of trophy, and on she marches with the troop, which is in truth the very victory she desires.

For her heart is torn with two passions, both of which could now have scope : a watchful jealousy of Tinnius, an admiration beyond all measure of Antinous.

Let Tinnius show any favour to any

Roman beauty, and Antinous shall match that beauty, or Boadicea is not Boadicea.

The Emperor rides out a few hundred yards to see that Segonax has recovered, and to say a few more words of temporary farewell to that Prince of Britons in the art of clay; and, having finished this act of condescension and good policy, follows in the wake of the cavalcade with Antinous and Tryphon as his companions, one on each side of him and both according to his own heart.

They march all day in this order, resting at night in a camp hastily pitched, but without one moment's hitch in the arrangements. The human machinery is as perfect as the order of the universe.

In this mode they advance rapidly to the north. Sometimes they call at a fixed encampment, a castrum, and remain for one or two days, but with few exceptions they make their own encampment and rest only one night.

They reach the great wall, they traverse its entire length, Hadrian giving forth his instructions, commending some parts of the work, and condemning other parts without reserve. Not a soul dares correct or suggest, and, good or bad, the work goes on according to his will.

The inspection completed, they return southwards, bearing to the east in order to reach Dola, the gate of the sea on a little island to the south-east side of the mainland, whence they may embark for Gaul, on their way to Rome. This march through Britain is most pleasant, and Hadrian in the first stages of it is as near to happiness as Hadrian possibly could be, and that is saying much for Hadrian.

For, in fact, this one of the greatest Cæsars is never favoured with felicity. A man of boundless energy without a trace of hope, he is worn out by what men call success more rapidly than hopeful men are worn out by failure.

He lives on his energy. So long as his mind is occupied with some new project, or study, or conversation, or difficulty, he is, to the world's eye, well and interested. So soon as the absorbing occupation is over he is, to his own heart, the most miserable man of all the hosts under his sway. A poor slave, lying on his straw dreading the morrow, may, by a gleam of hope, be a happy man compared with him for whose pleasure all slaves are prepared to minister.

Intrinsically, Hadrian is both good and great. He wears the purple as one born for it; he prizes it according to its worth, but he cares for it not the slightest. It gives him the means of employing himself as he likes, but it brings him no satisfaction. As to human pleasures, in their grosser sense, he knows nothing of them; what is called love he has never felt in its keen and absorbing passion of desire. Wine he looks upon as poison, and to him it is poison that would madden him unto death.

Field sports and games are too contemptible for his mind; state-craft does not afford variety enough for his eager faculties.

When he is moving he is most free of care, and knowing of this one remedy from sheer despair he is always a-foot; for years upon years he wanders through his empire, seeking rest and finding none.

One thing is greatly in his favour; he sleeps perfectly. The moment his simple evening meal is over and the brief interval of after-conversation has passed, he retires to his couch to sink into sleep like an infant. It is not the night, it is the morning he fears.

He wakes unrefreshed : he wakes as if he must sleep again, yet if he indulges in that desire his whole succeeding day is wearisome and sad ; he, therefore, rises with the sun, filled with sinking of the heart, hopelessness, and despair. Panic clutches him, some great impending evil, worse than the worst that could happen, is at hand, and is rendered still severer by the circumstance that the reality of it does not appear.

What shall he do? What shall he do? What shall he do?

The answer comes. Work! Work! Work!

He obeys, and soon, under his many manifold duties, all pursued with vigour, he regains serenity.

Tryphon, the physician of the school of the Asclepiades, has the confidence of Hadrian, simply because he has the divine art of seeing in what direction to treat his patient, so as to do as little as ever he can and yet always be doing something. If the Emperor thought there was anyone near him who didn't do something, woe be to that man.

Tryphon knows this, and easily fitting in his own life and ways to the life and ways of his master, is indispensable. He understands thoroughly the subtle disease from which his master suffers. Hippocates has told him all about it in an immortal essay on 'hypochondriasis.' He has learned the hour of each periodic attack, and is always at hand to meet it. He is there, not to listen to the tale of despair, but to offer some antidote in the way of information relating to the events of the coming day, where they are going and what they will see.

This is the cure of Tryphon. He knows it is a cure that must, in much shorter period than the natural period of the life of so strong a man as the Cæsar, bring even Cæsar to final repose; but it is, on the whole, the best cure, and prevents self-destruction.

In the new Antinous, the physician has found an ally of the best quality. Tryphon has no jealousies, and in this case he has all admiration. Antinous is of his own nation; has the same secret hopes as he in regard to that nation's deliverance from Rome; has the same reverence, with a more perfect knowledge of the Holy Scriptures of their race; has gifts which belong to no other race, and only to the most favoured of it; has youth, daring, skill, resource, beauty, beyond aught that is usually seen, and such command of presence as to be able to summon up into life any remaining latent power which any feeble son of earth can bring forth from what seems to be the abyss of death.

In all persons there is laid by a reserve of energy, a charge of vital tenacity which being evoked appears as a wonder, and to the unlearned as a miracle. In many this reserve power is altogether unknown until it is called forth by a will stronger than their own. Antinous has that stronger will, and when it is obeyed Antinous for the time excels so marvellously, that the deed is a miracle. The deed inspires belief, and by the very act of belief the doer is thought to be inspired.

In a sense this is true; Antinous holds more of the vital will than the majority of man or woman kind, a super-endowment amounting for all common observers to inspiration.

Hadrian, with the rest, has come under this spell, and in the many wonderful feats which his new companion performs with so much grace and power, forgets the sex, and treats Antinous as, in truth, a knight of Rome.

Henceforth, for a time, we will share with him in this happy delusion. Antinous shall be a knight of Rome.

Antinous rides with a mastery over every charger which continues to call forth admiration in all parts of the country they traverse. Sometimes, while the camp rests for meals, Antinous scours the country with perfect unconcern, to gather the news. Antinous has caught up with astounding facility the native tongues and dialects, converses with everybody, and confirms everybody in what they have heard of the mighty Emperor's marvellous powers. The cure of Segonax has spread abroad, and has so magnified by spreading that the people come to the feet of the Emperor bringing their sick that he may touch them, that they by the royal touch may be healed, and he, for a season, be happy.

To these arts Antinous adds faith, and Tryphon adds skill. Tryphon, at the bidding of the Emperor, extracts the head of a dart from the skull of a man who has been unconscious for many weeks. The dart removed, the unconscious man rises and begins to talk, but not in the language which his present friends understand.

The Emperor inquires does any one know where the man was born?

They answer, in Siluria. Then Antinous, who can speak to a Silurian, is fetched, and converses with the man freely. The man has regained his native, forgotten his acquired tongue. A native Silurian is found, who confirms the fact.

Miracle of miracles! the miracle of the camp of Eboracum in Northern Britain.

They march from Eboracum at quicker pace that they may not be impeded by too many intruders on their time, so says the wily Tryphon, who wishes to let success remain unsullied by any new experiment; and after a sharp series of marches southwards and eastwards they enter the splendid camp of Londinum, on the bank of the great river Thamesis that leads to the eastern sea.

In the course of this long and pleasant journey the knight Antinous has done many knightly wonders; but the choicest of these remains to be told. Antinous has vanquished completely Boadicea. That gallant virago, no longer viragoish, follows the knight with a simplicity that amounts to adoration. The beard of Tinnius has grown again, more resplendently than ever, but it has lost all its attractions.

The virago has no eyes, no heart, no soul except for Antinous.

As they enter Londinum there waits for them the Numidian Eli. It is sufficient for Boadicea to hate Eli because he singles out the noble knight of Rome for recognition as the cavalcade passes the gates of the camp. But when she sees that admirer enter the tent of the knight and receive commands, her jealousy knows no bounds. If the admirer were not so strong she would kill him. Yet a word from Antinous and all is right again; Eli is merely an attendant and a man.

The companions of Tinnius observe the change in his Boadicea, and rate him accordingly. Tinnius tugging his new beard, regales them with new wines, and stops all their raillery with new song and good humour. With all their banter they can neither make him jealous nor unhappy. On the contrary he, like the virago, worships Antinous.

Happy Antinous! Happy knight of Rome!

CHAPTER V.

THE NOVIOMAGIANS.

Towards the close of their journey from Eboracum to Londinum Hadrian is seized anew with one of the attacks of depression of mind which form so painful a part of his life. The road between the two great camps is one of the most level and perfect military highways in the whole of the empire, and in spite of his dejection he continues to admire it. But it is monotonous, and notwithstanding the speed with which they pass along it, it becomes, at last, very long and wearisome.

By the time he reaches Londinum the malady of depression has so much increased that it is a critical venture even to approach this master of the legions. He is ready to dispute on everything with everybody, yet he will bear no opposition. Those who oppose

him are open enemies; while those who too
easily give him his humour are secret conspirators.

Antinous chants to him some of her exquisite native poems and psalmodies translated
into purest Latin verse. He listens with a
sort of vacant wonder and pleasure, but it
does him no good in the end.

The wise Tryphon resorts at first to his
medicinal stores; he will administer helle-
bore. But when the suggestion is made to his
patient, the patient does not receive it with
confidence. Tryphon sees from his manner
that there lurks on the mind of the depressed
man an idea, common to his mental disorder,
that all about him are anxious to make away
with him, and that any drug which produces
decided symptoms would be suspected as a
secret or concealed poison.

Medicine consequently is given up for the
moment, and the next thing the wise physician
thinks of is some startling diversion. A hunt,
a race, a fight in the arena, a grand sail down
the noble river into the eastern sea. In vain!
in vain! Not one of these proposals receives
the slightest regard.

'If I could intensely divert him, and lift him out of himself for but one day,' Tryphon declares, 'he would possibly be cured. If I cannot he will soon crave to die.'

And all events in the world that Tryphon and Antinous most dread is the death of Hadrian. Let Hadrian die now and Julius Severus is Emperor without a doubt, and a great cause of theirs, ripening quickly into effective action, is lost for ever.

Israel must continue in chains if Hadrian dies.

In this dilemma the merry Tinnius Rufus, of all men least likely to give a prescription as these wiser heads think, comes in with one that is as gold to tin compared with all that has been suggested previously.

'Why not coax him to go to Noviomagus, the city and state of the new magicians?'

This is the prescription of Rufus the Redbeard.

While on the march Rufus has already told them some items about this singular place, and now he is asked more about it he tells them more.

Noviomagus is not farther than sixty stadii,

about eight British miles, a mere two hours' march, to the south-west of the camp at Londinum. It is mainly a Roman colony; its people, perfectly harmless, are great scholars and searchers into ancient mysteries and antiquities; but they have an extraordinary fashion, they do everything by contraries, and the results are rapturous.

The suggestion is splendid, but how is it to be carried out! Easily carried out. The citizen of Noviomagus who presides over the little community, as the Lord High President of the State, is a friend of Rufus, and has invited him to a banquet of the State which is the greatest peculiarity of all.

Why should not Hadrian, as a simple soldier companion in the camp of the Cæsar, go with him to the banquet?

The subtle Tryphon introduces the proposal to Cæsar with so much art that the plot is seized with actual avidity. He does not press Cæsar to go; he merely tells him about the place, and gradually intimates that Rufus in his jovial kind of way has said how droll it would be if the Emperor were to accompany him to the banquet, an event as unlikely as that a star should fall or a general earthquake break up all the earth.

The true word spoken in jest is, in this instance, proved to the letter; the day for the Noviomagian banquet arrives, and Rufus with a single companion, a common Roman soldier, is away on foot towards Noviomagus, the State of the new magicians.

The two cross the great river Thamesis in a galley, and making through a wooded plain begin to ascend a height from which the camp at Londinum is seen by them lying to the north-east in all its beauty.

The effect of the change on the mind of Hadrian is by this time well marked. The brisk exercise, the rattling tongue of Rufus, the newness of the scenery, the expectation of what is soon to come, have the best influence over the Emperor. It is as if a dense cloud were lifted from him; he begins again to like companionship, and to find a happier speech.

He becomes enthusiastic about the camp at Londinum. 'What a site it is,' he exclaims, ' for a mighty city, with that river equal to four Tibers at least flowing towards the ocean in such gallant style. One day this may become the emporium of the world.'

Rufus listens incredulously, but respectfully. He is glad to see the marked change in his master, and rattles away more merrily than ever. They make a little detour in order to avoid a camp to the east of them, and turning briskly round and marching nearly due west they come in sight of the temple or minor Parthenon dedicated to Minerva, which marks the centre of the Noviomagian territory, in the very heart of the Regni of Britain.

For some of the singularities of the Noviomagian citizens Hadrian has already been prepared. He has been advised that if he were forbidden the banquet ever so sternly he was still to take his place, because the more decisively he was forbidden the more eagerly was he welcomed. He is told that in Noviomagus every man holds an office except one who, representing every person not in office, is designated the Regular Citizen; and he is made fully conversant by his merry comrade with the grade and genius of every officer. No other story could have delighted so much the present childish mind of the Cæsar. It is school-boy days once more. He marvels what sort of men the Noviomagians will be to look at when he mixes with them. Will they really be grown-up men?

When at last he does meet them in the ante-room of the Temple, he finds them all grown-up men and very like other men of the graver Roman type; men well dressed, of good manners, and, when they choose, of learned speech.

Although Rufus is known to them all, they pretend not to recognise him, and order him and his doubtful friend away, with many curt and severe observations on their intrusive impertinence.

Tinnius Rufus and his comrade heed them not in the least. On the contrary, they make themselves quite at home, and assume, on their parts, that they are the masters of the situation, and that their hosts are impudent intruders into their domain.

The Noviomagians, charmed with the sublime impertinence of the soldier friend and companion of Rufus, ask aside of Rufus:—

'Who is this merry fellow of yours? Really who is he?'

And, amidst roars of laughter, Rufus answers in the plainest language he can speak.

'Cæsar.'

They accept, as the finest joke that ever has been played off in Noviomagus, this incredible reality, and at once in mock dignity address the stranger as if he really were Cæsar. Rufus trembles for a moment as having gone too far, but observing that the person most concerned is infinitely amused by it, and prepared to play out his part thoroughly, he keeps up the deception.

The banquet is served in the new fashion, with the guests sitting at the table, and Cæsar is put in the place of honour by the side of, and on the right hand of the Lord High President, the place designed for Rufus until this greater man was declared by Rufus himself.

At the close of the banquet the President, as a first duty, rises in his place, lights a taper which gives forth a pleasant odour and throws off rings of smoke as he waves it, and with all the company rising to their feet proclaims :—

'Saluti Augusti!'

'To the health of Cæsar!'

It is the common mode of reverence and recognition of the omnipresent Emperor from the time of Augustus Cæsar.

About this act of devotion there is no joke in Noviomagus; it is one of two serious parts of the Noviomagian performances. Hadrian is so much touched by the sincerity of this act that he conceals his real self with difficulty. For the first time since his elevation he has witnessed, behind his own back as it were, how he is reverenced.

He does not rise with the others to his feet. Splendid! 'Cæsar must not rise to Cæsar.' Of course not. He might have been a Noviomagian from his cradle, he plays his part so well.

Step by step he begins to learn, in detail, the names of all the great Noviomagian fraternity and their qualifications.

Ædes, the general in command of the forces of the State, is represented as having been selected to that office because of his surpassing peacefulness of disposition. He knows nothing of the soldier's art, and is so timid that he ran away the first and only time in his life when his courage was tested. The story is well told, but Hadrian sees through it and admires the spare generalissimo of the mimic state so much that if the wife and children of that hero were diviners they might forecast an anxious farewell in store for them.

Benignus, who combines in himself the two offices of Laureate and Treasurer, is, as his name implies, of benign and yet of merry countenance. Rufus approves him much, and all the company hold him in great reverence. On important occasions he writes a poem, and he is an entertainer of poets of other cities and countries. But his grand office in Noviomagus is that of collector of taxes and keeper of the State treasury. Of these taxes he refuses to give any record whatsoever. His word, he says, must be his bond.

By the laws of the State the Treasurer may be able to write, but he must not be able to read.

Crocus, the learned Recorder or Secretary of the State, is a very different personage. He is small, quick, and at the beginning serious. As time advances he becomes intensely witty, and his report of the last meeting is listened to by all with the utmost amusement. Crocus narrates the doings of the State well, but the best art he possesses is that of imitation of the style and manner of great orators, statesmen, poets, and princes.

By a fundamental law, it is ordained that the Recorder may be able to read, but he must not be able to write.

These particular laws, that the Treasurer must not be one who is able to read and the Recorder not one who is able to write, are of immense value. They prevent the Treasurer from reading up any extravagant ideas on the subject of political economy, and they prevent the Recorder from committing to paper or parchment any secrets or mysteries of the State, that ought to be concealed.

Balas, the Public Orator, has been originally elected to his post because of his utter inability to put two consecutive sentences together. Such, however, is the perversity of human nature that this Noviomagian, called Balas because he was at first only able to bleat out a little speech, has become, by the many calls made upon him to expound Noviomagian oracles, such a fine orator that there is now a standing notice for his dismissal from his post, which notice being marked 'urgent' is never brought forward.

Diventus the Architect of Noviomagus is described as the gravest man of all the assembly. It is his peculiarity that in the squares and gardens and parks of Noviomagus he keeps flocks of sheep, not for their flesh, nor for their wool, but as tests of salubrity. If the white fleeces of these animals become darkened by dirt and dust, he marks the spot where this change occurs as a spot fed by an air too impure to breathe. So the black sheep of the architect become proverbs, and the man who is about to take a house requires proof, before he concludes his bargain, that a spotless sheep has occupied the place for a lunar month without showing the slightest taint on its wool. The shearing of the sheep completes the bargain, and as each fleece sheared for this purpose is sealed up and placed in the record office as legal evidence of the transaction, a rather considerable institution has been developed amongst the public buildings.

The Keeper of the Public Records, including the wool-gathering records, is the learned Bulliens. The disturbance which his perpetual boiling over keeps up is most troublesome to the master of the feast, whose worst and wildest rulings meet with most favour, especially from the Censor Morum, one Rectus, a man of excruciating puns, never at rest, and whom the genial Hilarus, the Prefect or Sheriff of the State, cannot control, no, not even by better puns of his own.

Laurentius the high-priest of the famous temple, Phœnicius the traveller, Lyricus the minstrel, Peregrinus the pilgrim, and last but not least Patriarcha the venerable Father of the State, nearly as aged as Fidelis the centurion; these, surrounding and supporting the Summus Præses, the Lord High President of the State, form with the other citizens and guests a group as lively as it is inconsistent.

On the mind of Hadrian the many absurd stories, told without the least reserve, produce a mirthful rallying which adds to the curative effect his journey has produced.

He begins to reason on the inconsistencies until the inconsistencies become consistent.

'What,' says he to himself—' what a happy

sovereign of a future day that one will be who shall have a council or senate of the true Noviomagian type ; a secretary who cannot write ; a treasurer who cannot read ; a public orator who cannot speak ; a commander-in-chief who cannot set out troops ; or a general of the sea who has never boarded a ship ! '

In the course of fifteen or twenty centuries of civilisation even so strange an event as this may turn up in some centre of empire. If Londinum, so favourably placed on the great river, should expand into a mighty seat of government, why should not Londinum, so near to Noviomagus, attain to this perfection as it attains to its full development ?

The reflection only whets his thirst for more Noviomagian wisdom and practice, with which they ply him to any extent.

They do it practically. They proceed to take a vote on the question that Rufus, under the new Noviomagian name of ' Tristus ' (the sad), shall be admitted to citizenship. The vote unanimously says *no*, therefore Rufus is unanimously elected. This, the invariable rule of voting, is found to have many advantages, one of which was seen but a few weeks before, after a great debate on the question whether the state should go to war with a native chief called Getorix.

There was every reason why this marauder should be opposed, but the worst arguments, in opposition, carried the day, and the noes had it. Getorix thereupon marched unopposed on Noviomagus, and in crossing a river was lost with all his men.

In their public games the racer who, after doing his very best gets in last, is the winner, while he who, having tried his best, comes in first is the loser.

This principle holds good also in the schools, in the wrestling feats, in every competition; and, although at first sight it is opposed to common ideas, it is greatly in advance of all other methods, because no one is injured by it and the conceited are kept in their place.

In speaking of another person in Noviomagus, the rule is to praise the person named by relating the very opposite of what the world generally would say of his virtues, his vices, or his negative qualities. It is astonishing how well this answers. If a man is handsome he

is rated ugly, which subdues his conceit. If
he is hideous he is designated handsome,
which keeps him in good temper, a point of
enormous importance with all people whom
nature has made objectionable. A confirmed
rogue is treated as a singularly honest man,
under which device he is kept in honesty
more rigorously than by the discipline of fifty
strokes from the vitis.

If a man be by nature gifted with transparent falsehood, he is made proverbial for
his truthfulness. All men swear by his word.
'Mendax' was for many years thus honoured
throughout the State. All men swore by
Mendax, and his word was accepted as law. At
first Mendax relished the attention, but when
he found what it led to and the scrapes it got
him into, he changed altogether and became
such a confirmed pervert to the truth as to be
a nuisance from the insane exactitude with
which he related the most trivial anecdote, or
performed the most trivial service. At last,
having been put to determine whether the
colour of the sky, which all called blue,
was not green, he stuck to blue so pertinaciously that he ceased to be quoted as an

authority on anything and had to leave the place.

In like manner Pavo Maximo, who came direct from Rome and who was one of the most conceited asses that ever Rome sent forth, was greeted in Noviomagus with the profound reverence due to humility and power.

All Noviomagians encouraged Pavo to the utmost. They bade him think more of himself and less of them; they explained that he could not help being ill-favoured and feeble, because nature in her great designs ordains that such should be, and that the fault, of which he is innocent, is the natural retribution of the errors of his ancestors. In the brief space of two moons the effect of this wise and admirable encouragement was so telling on Pavo Maximo that, becoming a modest man, he sank into an obscurity which he singularly adorned, and his wife, enamoured of Noviomagus, presented him with offspring remarkable alike for their modesty and learning. In short, by this lucky stroke of statesmanship Noviomagus lost one foolish and gained five wise sons.

The hours pass happily away, and the

Lord High President of the State and the
Cæsar of Tinnius Rufus move on merrily
together. The Lord High is as frugal as his
guest, and like his guest touches no wine; but
raising a flagon filled with the purest of drinks,
the wine distilled by the sun and condensed
from the mountains by the Master of Life, he
proposes the other toasts or sentiments common
to the festival. He drinks to Noviomagus. He
informs his hearers that he is at peace with all
nations, and that he and the Cæsar exchange
the most friendly relationships, a statement
which the chief guest and his companion,
Tinnius Rufus, enthusiastically cheer, with a
sly look at each other which for the moment
so bewilders the Lord High, that he calls the
gods and the guests to witness the proof of
his assertion, from the fact of the presence of
the great potentate by his side.

Hilariously, the citizens pledge 'their noble
selves;' and then their leader calls upon them
to do the same to those members who for some
valid reason are not able to be present, des-
canting fully on the virtues of each absentee in
true Noviomagian humour.

He sits down to call on Lyricus to sing a

song which he, the Lord High, has composed
to go with this toast: whereupon Lyricus tunes
his lyre, and playing on it the accompaniment,
cheerfully obeys, in a melody as simple as the
words of the song :—

To Absent Friends.

We'll pledge our absent friends, dear friends,
    Our friendship true to prove;
And show to all that distance lends
    No distance to our love.

When from the sun the earth away
    Turns her retreating face,
Still burns the sun with brightest ray
    And still maintains his place.

And when from regions of the night
    The wearied earth doth stray,
Is there all beaming with his light
    To welcome her to-day.

Thus friendship true nor sinks nor sets,
    But always loves and lives.
The absent ones she ne'er forgets,
    Forgotten she forgives.

Then pledge our absent friends, dear friends,
    Our friendship true to prove;
And show to all that distance lends
    No distance to our love.

As the applause which follows the refrain

of the song ceases, the chief guest bids Tinnius Rufus get him the words for Cæsar.

Certainly. Cæsar shall have the words.

The Public Orator rises by command to recall the memory of the illustrious dead. Stephanus, their late Recorder, who has been received into the number of the gods, is the chief departed memory. Him Noviomagus ever mourns, and is now erecting a monument to his fame ; but others also are named, with cheerful pathos and affectionate remembrance.

For a time the scene changes. The guests are told that for an interval mirth will give way to serious discourse. The Lord High President has the full power to appoint one of his officers, or one of the guests, to relate some veritable experience or fact that shall at once prove pleasant and instructive. This time he commissions Phœnicius, who has long been absent on his travels, to tell of his adventures.

Phœnicius, of true Phœnician birth and accomplishments, relates thereupon his latest travel, to which the one particular guest listens with rapt attention.

Phœnicius has sailed to an island in the far northern sea, in which island there is perpetual night and perpetual day for months at a time ; in which the sparse population spend almost a winter of sleep ; in which the cold is so severe that at periods the island is a 'rock of ice'; but in which, nevertheless, there are springs of boiling water shooting up from the ground many feet high.

'If this is not Noviomagian,' observes Tinnius Rufus, as Phœnicius concludes, ' it is so near to it I see not the difference.'

And he laughs till his fat cheeks tremble like two jellies.

The effect on his companion is of a serious kind. He asks for more information. In what direction is this island? How distant is it? Is the sailing to it easy? Are the inhabitants fierce or gentle? Who is king or chief of it? Have the Romans ever been there? Has any Roman or Greek author described it? Did Phœnicius understand the language of the people? Have the hot springs any medicinal value?

These and fifty more questions are asked of Phœnicius with eager inquiry, and answered by him with his natural courtesy and keen intelligence.

Why should a common soldier of the army, one who is not even a centurion, want to know so many things about the distant northern island?

The soldier is set down as a very intelligent soldier.

'Are all the soldiers who serve in the body-guard of Cæsar as interested in these subjects of travel as yourself?' inquires the Lord High of his guest.

'Not all, but some are?'

'They reflect the mind of their Imperial master,' continues the innocent speaker.

The guest reddens, and Rufus pales. The conversation is getting uncomfortably warm.

'Ask him to sing,' suggests Rufus as a diversion; 'he has a good voice, and is fond of the art.'

The Lord High President is charmed with the idea, and in a moment or two is able to tell the citizens that amongst the other accomplishments of the Cæsar of Rufus there is a voice that can sing.

Will their guest give them a taste of his

melody? The Cæsar of Rufus, the common soldier of Rome, will be delighted to obey the Lord High President and his loyal people. It is the duty of every soldier to obey his sovereign. Can they favour him with a lute?

A lute is brought. It is tuned by the performer, who loves to show off his musical skill, with a touch, and ear, and grace which surprises Noviomagus.

Could a common soldier tune a lute like that?

Rufus, seeing the puzzle, solves it by whispering something which goes quickly round the table:—

'His mother was a famous musician.'

The instrument is attuned, Noviomagus listens, and Cæsar with sweet voice sings, in words and music all his own, the song subjoined.

My Heart's Desire.

What is my heart's desire?
  To know! to know!
Whence comes the living fire
That in my breast doth glow
  And whither it must go.

What is my heart's desire?
  To sit on high,

And like a god aspire
  To conquer destiny,
    As one who cannot die.

What is my heart's desire?
  To lay up gold,
Such riches to acquire
And such possessions hold
  As cannot all be told.

What is my heart's desire?
  A woman's love,
Sweet as a well-tuned lyre,
True as the star above
  Round which all others move.

What is my heart's desire,
  Above all these?
A friend who will not tire
Of friendship's subtleties,
  Though all my faults he sees.

As the last touch of the lute dies away Noviomagus rises, perfectly entranced with the voice, the style, and the matter of the singer, who is soon again absorbed in the gossip and various amusements which prevail.

The hours pass, for once at least, merrily with Hadrian.

Crocus the Recorder and mimic of mimics has skilfully got up the Cæsars, their manner of life and various styles of speech.

He is called upon to 'play the fool,' and he does it in this representation.

He begins with Julius Cæsar haranguing his troops; he passes to Augustus finishing the comedy of his life; Tiberius defending debauchery; Caligula feeding horses on golden oats; Claudius making love to Agrippina; Nero reciting the fall of Troy; Galba hiding his money-bags; Otho praying to be allowed to die; Vitellius the glutton ordering his dinner; Vespasian making the young nobles march barefoot; Titus bargaining with Josephus the Jew; Domitian killing flies with a pin; Nerva selling his old clothes and imperial robes for the good of the State; Trajan having his head shaved by a supposed conspirator; and lastly, Hadrian disputing with Favorinus in defence of luxury over a bunch of sorrel, a crust of dry bread, and a cruet of vinegar.

From humour to sadness, from genial satire to genial praise, from wisdom to the extremest folly, the merry Recorder of Noviomagus leads his friends along. Happy for him, as Rufus keenly feels, his criticism on the last Cæsar is to the very shade what the last Cæsar could hear of himself, not only without offence but sitting unchanged and looking up at the orator with a face of as true levity, kept under control, as the orator himself maintains.

'So much for Cæsar,' cries out the Recorder as he resumes his place, to the applause of all around.

The mirth still continues, jokes abound; tales of all kinds and countries and persons are exchanged, and the last of the formalities is about to be carried out.

The Lord High President of Noviomagus has risen in his place to pledge the health of the Cæsar of Rufus, of Tinnius Rufus himself, and the other renowned Visitors, when a scene altogether unprecedented takes place.

An intrusion into the banqueting hall of Noviomagus!

Impossible!

'Nay, my Lord High President,' says the pale and breathless messenger who bears the news, 'it is true; there are those outside who will enter and whose business admits of no hindrance. They threatened to run me through with their swords if I came not with this paper to Cæsar.'

Taking the whole affair as a Noviomagian joke, the Lord High President amidst a roar of laughter receives into his own hands the massive dispatch and transfers it with profound mock solemnity to the mysterious guest, by whose side the lute still lies.

The dispatch bears an inscription 'From Rome,' and the seal or signet appended to it is the seal of the Senate of that mother of empires.

The joke is superb, even in Noviomagus.

It must be the work of Hortensis the regular citizen of Noviomagus who, conspicuous by his absence since the first part of the banquet, has been concocting this huge surprise as a sly compliment to the companion of Rufus.

Cæsar himself receives the document in the same jovial spirit, but as his eye glances over it his countenance changes.

Like a flash, the face of the merry soldier is transformed into the dignity of the stern and mighty Imperator.

'Who brings this missive?' he exclaims in a voice of authority and thunder.

Noviomagus is bewildered. The red face

of Rufus becomes pallid; the Lord High President hesitates, but the rest of the company, accepting the speech and action as magnificent comedy, cheer and laugh the more.

Taking no heed of their noise, the receiver of the dispatch breaks the seal and reads the epistle.

We who are allowed to read it with him may tell the message.

It is a message from the Senate to Cæsar the absolute. It prays, it all but insists, for his instant return to Rome. An insurrection of the Jews in Cyprus has led to a threatened universal rising in Palestine, which nothing less than the immediate presence of the Emperor can prevent.

The Emperor reads, reflects a moment, and with peaceful manner amounting even to tenderness speaks:—

'Citizens of Noviomagus, and henceforth all of you knights of Rome, know that it has been your fate to make Cæsar happy. But Cæsar has duties that call him home, and Tinnius Rufus, from this night Governor of Palestine, is required also at his post. Nay, move not, I pray you, for one moment from your mirth, but heartily let Cæsar thank you as he says farewell.'

The Noviomagians rise still half incredulous, as Cæsar, attended by Rufus, is about to retire from the hall in the wake of the messenger.

Is it credible; have they been entertaining Cæsar after all?

The bent knee of the President, as he kisses the hand extended with imperial dignity towards his lips, the noise of horsemen without the walls, and the royal submission of the new Governor of Palestine make, at last, the incredible the credible.

They all bend, and Cæsar departs, yet not without one last look round as he reaches the portico leading into the outer court; one more graceful recognition; and, one more *vale*— farewell; followed by a shout from Noviomagus that is deafening:—

'*Ave Cæsar!*'

They would have rushed out in a crowd, but the returning messenger tells them it were in vain. An escort of soldiers, he relates, was at the door. Two dismounted were holding the horses for the two who have left the table, and these latter mounting the steeds have in one moment galloped, in the midst of the escort, along the way to Londinum.

The two remaining soldiers, centurions both of them, are left by Cæsar to the care of Noviomagus until the morning.

They are received with a warmth and welcome which is as new to their life as it is pleasant to their tastes. They take the places lately occupied by Cæsar and Rufus. They are treated to food, and fruit, and wine. They turn out, when all restraint is off them, to be true soldiers, as mirthful as they are resolute. They tell their stories about the long marches they have had with Hadrian for two years past. They describe the scene of the Jew and the Numidian bear; the festival in honour of Fidelis and the death and cremation of that hero; the character of Julius Severus; the influence of Antinous and all else they have seen, with a simple frankness that wins for them the greatest admiration.

The Public Orator descants on them so eloquently that at last he is, by necessity, deposed from his office; the Laureate tries an extempore poem *re* Cæsar ; the Recorder reads from a blank parchment a minute chronicling events, which the Keeper of the Public Records undertakes faithfully to preserve ; the Censor Morum perpetrates a pun on the word centurion, which is too bad to be worth noticing ; and the Architect finishes by constructing for the guests ' a bed of thorns ' on which they sleep as they have never slept before in all their memory.

CHAPTER VI.

LOVE AND LEVIATHAN.

It is time that we should return to our travellers, whom we left to their repose in the natural palace which they had discovered on their way to the western sea of Britain.

We rejoin them there when their sojourn is concluded, refreshed and recruited with food, and ready for their journey.

By this time they so well understand each other that they are as one family. Towards Simeon the fair Erine Leoline—to repeat her beautiful name—feels no restraint. It is to her as if she had known him all her life. She has a pre-existent sentiment that long ago she knew him, and that by some strange and affectionate tie she was so attached to him that they were veritably the same persons in heart, in mind, in soul.

To a wise and inquiring man this idea

would evoke points upon points of controversy. But Erine Leoline does not pretend to be wise, is not inquiring on such subtle matters as mental phenomena, and is as far from being a man as any one of her sex can be.

Leon, her father, is also affected towards the youth beyond mere passing favour. What was at first sympathy has passed into responsibility. The youth is to Leon like the raised embodiment of his own child who died, or, as he would say, was translated at birth.

This impression had flitted across the mind of Leon even as they journeyed, and now that he has read the book of fate which the youth carries on his bosom there is no hesitation. Leon has not simply surmised, he has read and interpreted his duty.

As the shadows of the evening begin to fall they prepare themselves for their further journey, and soon depart on their way.

Yet they turn to look back at the beautiful palace of nature which they have occupied for one day, and as they look they linger.

For now the palace is in all the glory of sunset. It is filled with a rich, ruddy sunset glow. Its central mound, permeated and cleft through, yields the most wonderful shadows: its splash is in sweeter tune than ever; the birds are returning to their nests, and in the caves dark shades fill the spaces.

It is hard to turn away, but they must be gone. One more glance, Erine Leoline; one more glance, Simeon, the running torch; one more look into that palace of nature, and one look athwart each other's eyes ere your faces turn into the future.

Into the dark, dark eyes of thine, Simeon, how deep those blue eyes of thy maiden companion sink! Thou hast in thine heart, strong youth and king, two wells of life from which thy rich blood springs. Thither, thither those blue eyes have sent their searching rays, and left them there.

Under the first impression, so deeply set, the heart of Simeon well-nigh stands still; then it quickens; it beats in his throat; it vibrates to the end of every nervous fibre; it fills his breast with fire; it flushes his eyes till tears are wanted to give relief.

Thou art charged with fire, Simeon, with new and living and immortal fire. And thou, gentle Erine, thou has lost what he has gained.

Sweet maiden of maidens, how pale thou art! how thine heart also doth flutter with sweet tumultuous bliss at loss of the treasure thou hast given up for ever! Is it faith that supports thee, sweet child, so that thy colour returns? Is it fear of having too impulsively lost what thou canst never recall that makes thy pale cheek glow with the virgin blush of beauty?

It is both : it is faith and fear ; but faith prevails.

Their hands touch as they turn from the past into the future. It is the faintest of touches, yet is it a thrill through all their natures, body, soul, and spirit ; a thrill of felicity such as they have never felt before, and never in the same intensity and richness shall feel again.

To no mortal born, man or woman, is it given to taste that ecstatic thrill twice in this mortal life.

The young lion and the lioness have met, and a little child could lead them. They are led by one of childish purity and giant manliness ; so safe a guide as few can hope to follow.

Their course from this time is westward, on the upper margin of a forest, with a valley on their right hand, and the moon and stars as their light. With the rising of the sun, the philosopher once more ascends a favouring height, takes his observations, makes and exchanges his signals, satisfies himself as to the route he must pursue, and returning with his children into the forest, discovers for them all a shelter, in which they pray, and eat, and take once more their rest.

Refreshed and ready for travel they start again, and coming to an ascent which they climb, see before them in greater width and in silvery beauty the stream or river which they had before beheld in the distance as a mere streak of bright and shining metal. It seems so near, the young people think they must surely reach it in one short stage, but in this idea they are corrected by their guide, who impresses on them patience and persevering progress.

In this the last stage to their destination they pass once more into forest land. They are now in a deep and wooded valley, where once the sea had its bed at the mouth of a bay of great extent. They wind their way through natural paths, in the midst of rocks on dry land. The rocks take the most fantastic shapes. There is a triangular cave of rock in which fifty people might stand, and from one angle of which is an opening into the air above, where, as they discover, man has once found a temporary home, for the walls show the effects of fire and smoke. There is a huge rock many cubits in circumference, and of the height of twenty full-grown men standing on each other's shoulders, yet resting, vast as it is, by a narrow neck on quite a little rock beneath it, so that it seems as if it would topple over by the faintest wind. There is a projecting rock like the prow of a vessel, and another like the stern of a vessel. They mount a height by a set of natural steps, and coming upon a stony crest see, standing out in the midst of a glade of trees, a great boulder, shaped like a human head, on which the rude native sculptors have cut a hideous face, a demon of evil, fierce, merciless and devouring. They start by their footsteps a hawk from her nest, and see her fly away into the depth beneath, leaving one of her helpless young in the ferns at their feet. Simeon catches the little bird and gives it, savage as it is, to the gentle hands of Erine, who, admiring its big black eyes while dreading its sharp and powerful beak, soothes it so gently that it lies on her bosom without fear. She fondles it, kisses it, and putting it back into its nest with a final caress, joins her father and Simeon in descending into the glade.

They pass under an arch of rock carved like honeycomb on its exquisite roofing and columns; and, in time, they arrive at a little bay, walled in with trees so closely that there seems, at first sight, to be no outlet for the smallest craft, but at the bottom they find an outlet which brings them to the shore of the great river.

On the margin of this haven of repose they watch and rest. A path of smooth grass with shelving sides to the water might tempt them to march westward, but their leader knows his duty; he tells them to wait here, and he is willingly obeyed. What is waiting, or time, or space, in a first day's love?

Simeon and Erine know nothing of waiting, of space, of time. To themselves space and time are, as they are to themselves, one, and all in all.

In some recesses of Simeon's memory the details of a tragic life must needs be treasured up. His early career in the desert of Carmel; his wanderings with the wonderful man who nurtured him as his own child; his education under that consummate master; his residence in Cæsarea and a marvellous event there that brought him, in Roman charge, to distant Britain; his trial here; his awful conflict and victory when death was close at hand; his more awful ordeal of fire, and even still more miraculous escape; all these facts must be treasured up in his memory.

And his long and true companion, now lost to him, the centurion of a hundred years, the faithful Fidelis, he surely must ever be in memory?

Above all, that true and holy woman, inspired to do what no other woman he has ever known could do. She who would most willingly lay down her life to save him, who has filled his soul with her own inflaming zeal; she who has sung to him the sweet songs of Israel; prophesied to him his future glory ; she who can cast out evil spirits.

She, bearing the signs and seals of a divine mission, cannot fail to be in his memory at every moment, though all else be absent.

Not at this moment. No! Not one of them is present with him in memory now.

He and Erine are seated on the trunk of a fallen tree, and Leon the wise, always questioning nature, reminds them, as he tries to solve it for himself, of a problem that rose in his mind, as they passed through the valley of rocks and discovered bodies of large gnarled and wildly shaped trees springing out of hard rocks as if they were a part of the same, together with little ferns and tender plants springing from similar hard and barren soil.

How did the seeds of those living forms, little and great, first take root? On what do they thrive? How do they draw their food and water from so unlikely a source?

His listeners hear, yet do not heed: the rustle of their palpitating hearts confuses their reason.

As some thoughtless or rude nature stricken

by words that reach its heart undergoes what is called conversion, and becomes a new creature, so these natures, gentle, courageous, youthful, have undergone a conversion equally instant, deep, and incisive; the conversion of love.

What to them is the past, or all that it contains? What the present, with its knotty problems of trees growing out of stones?

What the future?

They in their very rhapsody stop there.

By some hidden, bottomless mystery they link their future with their present. The future, unrecognisable as time, indescribable as love itself, is inscrutably connected with them and their rhapsody.

It feels to them both as something not before them; a distance without an horizon; a scene without a single object; a period that is an eternity.

Could they both die, would they not still live?

That child Erine, until a few hours ago, knew herself only as a child. In her whole being she understood but one affection for one person who absorbed all persons, the father who now sits musing on trees growing out of rocks. My philosopher, there is a harder puzzle even than that to solve close by thy side. This child of thine has become by some miracle a woman. She loves thee still; but —oh fearful *but*—she loves some one else deeper than she loves thee.

Thou hast nursed her, shielded her, fed her, clothed her, taught her, carried her in thy strong yet gentle arms, soothed her to sleep, waked her with the pure kiss of fatherhood, been to her more than thou wert ever to thyself.

On thee from her first look until now her eyes have been set, on none so often and so long. If thou wert absent for a brief period how those eyes would weep lest she had lost thee! When thou didst return, how those eyes would lighten with joy and those feet carry her to thee until she was clasped in thy embrace!

Those lips how they hung on thine! how often have those hands beguiled thee into quiet nooks and corners, that thy voice might pour into her ears of pearl some tale of childish marvel told and retold again and again and again!

Those looks and expressions of admiration trust, gratitude; how often hast thou tasted them and lived on them as on angels' food?

It has been all true, great philosopher, musing on trees growing on rocks; but think thou of this problem; unravel it, and thou art wiser than if thou discernest food in stones.

Why is it, as it truly is, that this thy child, bone of thy bone, flesh of thy flesh, this child whom thou hast cherished on richest soil of love, would leave thee and cleave unto him whom but three days ago it had not entered her mind to conceive as living either in earth or heaven?

A rock, philosopher, may nourish a tree, but answer thou this, what nourishes the love of a maiden for the man on whom she has transplanted her love? For aught she knows, it may be a rock on which it is transplanted, yet will it grow there even as the trees and slender plants in the rock land of the forest.

It is a terrible fact, too, that the transplantation of the love shall be so complete as to leave thee practically childless.

Nay, weep not and wonder not. It is the will of thine own goddess, Nature. What cares

Nature for thee or thy heart? She wills that the race shall live, not thou alone.

And, if she did not will that thy child should leave thee and cling unto another, the living world would stop to-morrow.

Who art thou, man, that should stop the world of life? Whatever thou art, wise as Solomon, strong as Hercules, the world must go on.

No man is more likely to understand this hard lesson to the very bottom of it than Leon the wise, when his eyes are open to receive it.

As yet he is meditating on the subject of trees growing out of rocks, and much study, like much love, or rather much study with much love, makes him blind.

The lovers, for lovers they are now, signed and sealed by fate, though they know it not in all its fulness, rise and wander along the grassy beach crushing the stones and sand with their feet, and with slow pace, as if divining from the earth some secret they want to know and which the earth will not reveal to them.

Their eyes are cast down, but their hopes are high, and their minds are in the sweetest unrest.

It is very curious that they do not speak the one to the other.

Have they been stricken dumb?

They are moving upwards in regard to the stream, so that its brisk and full current faces them. Suddenly, with a cry of great joy, Erine discovers, floating down the stream, something which she recognises.

Simeon sees something also, but what is it?

It must be the great Leviathan of which he has read; and, indeed, what else can it be, for its ' eyes are like the eyelids of the morning, out of his nostrils goeth smoke, the flakes of his flesh are joined together, the arrow could not make him flee; he makes the sea boil like a pot, he makes a path to shine after him!'

It must be Leviathan!—Leviathan that can never be taken by the hand of man.

It passes them swiftly, and they turn to follow it until they reach the spot where they had left their guide, by some waft of whose hand the huge monster stops in its course.

Erine claps her hands with delight. Simeon stands as one petrified with surprise.

The monster moves by the mere finger-guidance of Leon ; now it backs a little up the stream ; then it makes a sidling to the shore where they stand ; again it backs up the stream ; once more it sidles in until it is within a few feet of them. Then along its mighty backbone it splits atwain, and behold the deck of a boat of oriental splendour!

The covering arch, divided into two parts, is slipped down on each side so as to become the bulwarks or sides of the vessel, and a platform pushed across to the shore allows the travellers to step on board as though they were traversing a bridge of dry land.

For a moment Leon hesitates, as if about to carry his beloved child in his arms across the little bridge, when, lo! she has escaped, and with her face alight with rapture is beckoning not him, Leon, but Simeon, towards the deck of Leviathan.

For the first time the study of the trees and the rocks leaves the mind of Leon the Wise for the study propounded above. He sighs and says nothing.

As they enter on the deck some strains of music welcome them. The crew come merrily up to greet them ; the captain and his officers are in ecstasy at their coming, and everything is ready for their arrival. Yet two things embarrass them : the presence of the stranger and the demeanour of their master, Leon the Wise. For a deep silence has fallen on Leon, such as they have never before known.

Hitherto when he has rejoined them he has been full of questions, has traversed every part of the vessel, looked at every rope, anchor, instrument; called for the book of events, and, hand in hand with Erine, has spoken to every soul on board.

Now, with a general gentle recognition of them all, he passes into his chamber or cabin with a subdued and saddened expression on his noble face.

And Erine, how changed she is! On the deck one of the chief officers planned some few months before a swing, into which he has been accustomed to lift her, and, starting her off buoyant and light, has kept up the motion until she herself has asked that she may 'die down.' During her late absence he has done up the swing afresh, has decorated it splendidly, has added to its height, has furnished it with a cord by touching which she can keep the swing in motion by her own sweet will. With the aid of three or four men he commences to erect the swing so soon as the deck is open, and now it is ready for use.

Can it be believed? So changed is she, he wishes he could drop the swing below the deck. Lift her into it as he would have done a month ago! Absurd idea. She gives him a gracious hand and smile as she passes rapidly to her cabin, but the swing is quite unheeded.

The child has become a woman!

She too retires into her own apartment or cabin and remains there.

Before they begin to comment on these strange changes, Simeon attracts and diverts their attention. To him the scene has a freshness he cannot too closely grasp and hold. He is even now almost of opinion that he is in the body of some gigantic sea animal inhabited by a spirit which animates and governs it; and he is not far wrong, for the marvellous builder of this craft has taken the body of a Leviathan for his model, has built upon it on even a larger scale, and has filled it with his own governing mind and reasoning soul.

The interpreter of the crew, who can speak

all known tongues, converses with him freely in Hebrew, Greek, or Latin, Greek seeming easiest to both of them, for Simeon knows Ionic Greek intimately, and Goscius, the learned and handsome interpreter, is a Greek by birth and education, and such a scholar of languages as none but a Greek can be.

Led by his new friend they pass through all parts of Leviathan, by which name, so slightly modified the difference is not worth noting, the vessel is really called. They pass to the lower decks; they descend to a place where the sailors, by working a pump which causes water to lift a lever, set in motion an archimedean screw, under which the vessel can be moved at the will of the commander. He is shown the air-chambers, which, as in Leviathan the living, can be charged with air to feed the crew should they wish to close in and descend under water. He is shown how, by letting in and letting out water, the vessel can be raised or lowered at pleasure into the water. He is taught by what an instant and simple plan the back of Leviathan is closed or opened. He is led to the stores of food and grain; to the place where the foods are cooked and made ready for use. Then he is led to the treasury or bank, entirely under the control of Goscius, where all coins and valuables are kept, and is shown every kind of money suitable for commerce in every nation they may visit.

The survey altogether opens up to Simeon a new world, in which two facts stand over and above all. There is not in the whole community of the Leviathan a single secret place or key, or spot where anything can be hidden; and there is not one single weapon of offence or defence on any person or on any wall or part of the vessel.

On the contrary, all here is arranged for human knowledge and human pure delight. Musical instruments are abundant, books and pictures are everywhere, strange mechanical contrivances lie about, and on the lower deck there is a veritable museum of natural curiosities, the cleaning and setting and ordering of which is a part of the work of all who are on board. Erine has her cabinet of precious shells and stones; Goscius his of coins and metals; Leon his of mechanical models; and there are many more.

Simeon, if he stays, will have to make up a cabinet of some kind like the rest.

If he stays? Why, of course, he must stay. Where else has he to go? and if he had, how could he be so ungenerous as to leave his preservers? Besides, what would Erine say?

There is, moreover, something about this crew that fascinates him, spell-binds him. Their picturesque dresses of pure white, edged with gold and held round the body with loose silken scarves of red; their purple headgear, shaped like the broad leaf of a plant, flat on the crest of the head and with the point slightly overhanging the brow; the richly-laced sandals; the smartness, good nature, and beauty of the men themselves. All these peculiarities fascinate him, and well they may. In other vessels in which he has lived things were done in an orderly way, no doubt, but with much shouting, noise, and decided unwillingness on the part of every man to do any more than his own appointed duty. Here every man does everything that is required at the moment without hesitation, so that order and comfort and cleanliness are universal habits and universal benefits.

As the mind of Simeon gets attuned to the scenes around him he becomes conscious of his own singularity. He must be out of harmony in his soiled and scorched and torn garb, so different to theirs who are guiding him about.

Struck with this discovery he apologises to the friendly Goscius, who, appreciating his difficulty, proceeds at once to remove it by leading him to the strangers' cabin and supplying him with every garment and every facility that shall enable him to robe in unison with the rest of the crew.

Like a child getting new clothes, Simeon fits himself out for his part. He refreshes himself with the bath; he arrays himself in his new garments. Surely Solomon in all his glory was never more sumptuously, never more comfortably attired.

In his bright apparel he seems to have assumed a brighter nature; his footstep is more elastic, his body more erect, his limbs more powerful and free. The merry attendant who ministers to his wants looks on with great admiration.

Thus rehabilitated he returns to the main

deck a new man, taller than any other man there, slightly taller than Leon, and in mien, manner, and build the most majestic of all.

No wonder that the sweet Erine has developed so rapidly into a woman!

From the richly cushioned seats at the stern of the vessel, which is now ploughing along the river towards the western sea, Erine and Leon rise to receive their guest. Leon is clothed like his friends: Erine has nearly the same attire, but has added to it, for the first time in all her life, the light mantle of womanhood—her mother's mantle, laid by for many, many, a long year, and now brought forth as a sign to him, whose child she is, that she is no longer a child.

Leon knows his loss at last; he recalls the trees and tender plants growing out of the rocks So from henceforth must his love grow.

So shall it be.

He remembers how from her parents he stole the love that came to him from her whose mantle has fallen to-day on the shoulders of his own, his only child. He sees the robber who this time comes to him as he once came himself. Perhaps there is a secret pang in that moment of hesitation before he rises; but, if so, it is for no longer than a moment, and is covered by the brightness of his voice as he bids his princely guest ' welcome to Leviathan.'

The princely guest kneels his acknowledgment with exquisite grace and dignity.

Is it all gratitude and homage, or is there mixed with it the trembling hope that the hand of the matchless Erine will help him to rise?

If there were such a trembling hope it need give him trouble no longer, for it is realised in full as he rises and stands in radiant joy with her hand in his and with her angelic face uplifted towards his own.

Their gaze must be longer than they imagine, for when it is over Leon has departed from them and they are alone.

With tremendous force of torrent foaming to the sea they pass as they stand, all in all to themselves, the ruin of a Roman pharos or lighthouse, and roused from their reverie by the voices of the crew, they cast up their eyes to see on the crest of that pharos a solitary man who waves to them his hand.

The Numidian bear!

But how changed! dressed now as a Roman, and wearing on his head the cap of liberty.

The sweet Erine, filled with affright, sinks on the breast of Simeon as if to shield him from an evil spirit, and he sustains her there as if his life depended on her protection. But towards his former foe he feels so little fear and such strong regard, he calls out for Leviathan to stop that the stranger may be taken on board.

His voice is not heeded, for at this moment there is seen coming up the stream in face of them a fearful wave which, like a wall of water in ramparts, will overwhelm them.

In an instant Leviathan closes, sinks, dives beneath the wall of many waves, and when they return to the surface, a mile at least away, the lonely occupant of the pharos is visible no longer.

But standing still, wrapped in that fast and long and sweet embrace which knows no time and feels no shame, they become conscious of another form which has approached them lovingly, and has called them both his children, the children of Leon the Wise.

Between them another new love is born. A son long lost has been restored to Leon, in whom son, and daughter never lost, are absorbed as one.

It is a new love, but precious as the old and boundless as the open sea which Leviathan is now about to breast and to conquer.

CHAPTER VII.

ANTINOUS AND FAME.

WE may with advantage rest for a brief moment here, in order to explain what was the nature and the import of the news which caused Hadrian to leave the Noviomagians so hastily and anxiously, and why the Senate should so eagerly demand his return to the heart of the empire.

There is sedition amongst the Jews.

The Jews are a conquered people. Long before this time Vespasian and Titus drove them out of their Holy City, laid bare and laid low their Holy of holies, scattered them like chaff before the wind into the different quarters of the wide earth, and planted the Roman standard over the strongholds of Palestine.

Moreover, these rulers, their predecessors

and their successors, have planted Roman money in every market and store, the strongest proof that Cæsar is everywhere. When men carry the head of Cæsar, in metallic casting, in the pouches of their dress and find that head passing for the purchases of life, there Cæsar must reign if anybody reigns at all.

To all external signs and proofs Cæsar reigns, beyond a shadow of a doubt, over Palestine and over every man in it.

Let a Jew try the question and see how he likes the answer. Let him declare himself a Pharisee, a Sadducee, an Essene, a Nazarene, a Gnostic, an Ebionite, or any other of the then prevailing Jewish sects, and let him, in declaration and defence of his faith, refuse to burn incense to Cæsar!

He will not forget the refusal, even if he survive it. Our own Simeon is a proof sufficient of this fact.

The present Cæsar, Hadrian, has no particular care about sects, nor, in a personal sense, any care whatever about the adoration paid to him as a man. He is an Athenian scholar, versed in philosophy, admitted to the highest degree of philosophy as an archon, a friend of the great teachers of the Athenian schools, including Aristides himself, and is above all vindictive passions about sects and doctrines pure and simple. To Fortunatus he writes respecting the great centre of learning, Alexandria, that the place is made up of Jews, Samaritans, Christians, and worshippers of the Egyptian deities, but that in the midst of their contests and quarrels about their faiths 'the sects worship, in reality, but one god, and that god is money.'

Hadrian, therefore, has no religious feeling against the Jews as Jews. On the contrary, he is rather smitten with the Gnostic culture which some of them have supported and developed, the refined mysteries and exalted hopes of that culture being well attuned to his poetic mind. But when Rome is challenged, and when Hadrian as Emperor is defied, then the Cæsar breaks forth with all the fire of Cæsar. Then from what seems, and what ordinarily is, a mild and gentle man there issues the most fearful vengeance, tempered only by a sense of fear and superstitious dread of some power mightier than his own, which does not disdain, any more than he himself disdains, to manifest itself through human agency.

The Jew under the rule of Hadrian is, therefore, whatever his sect may be, perfectly safe if he conforms to Roman law and is ready to show his subjugation by lawful homage to the chosen Head of the Roman Power. But woe be to him if his lawful homage fail.

The Jews are a conquered race? No! so long as one human pair remains to keep a race alive, a race is never conquered. So they believe, and they are right. Hadrians never so many may beat them, punish them, burn them, crucify them, degrade them; let that one solitary pair, from which the race can be continued, remain, and that race may yet have its turn and conquer all the Hadrians and their followers.

Did not Adam and Eve, one pair, people the world?

The Jews at this time have many thousands of human pairs who will pair with none out of their own race. They are borne down by numbers and by Roman discipline, but conquered? Never.

Hadrian of all men knows and feels this

truth ; knows it better than the Senate that has sent for him. The Jewish line of people is to him like a worm which you may divide with a sharp instrument, and out of every divided part a new and perfect organisation will grow.

In addition to this knowledge he is filled with a superstitious dread of this chosen people. Their God is a God of battles, and in his might, majesty, and ultimate dominion they have a confidence which nothing can shake. Their belief is born in them, and has come down in the stream of generations. They know that their God will never leave them nor forsake them; punish them, yes; let them feel their own weakness for a time, yes. But leave them, forsake them! Never. They are his flock and the sheep of his pasture.

They are, too, a wise people. In craft and subtlety the Roman hordes are to them as so many blocks of wood and stone. Even he, Hadrian, a Spaniard with not a drop of Roman blood in his veins, but with some ancient Egyptian blood there, is no match for them. Their rod eats up his rod, as in the days of the

Pharaoh. What they cannot do by strength they will do by subtlety.

Worst of all, to him, they are, as he believes, an inspired people. They can perform what others can do no more than hope for. This mighty One of theirs, who governs above all Joves and Junos and Roman deities, deigns to fill with some part of his own omnipotence certain of these chosen of his chosen. What evidence of this fact could be clearer than is afforded in this new Antinous, his matchless attendant in disguise, who can cast out devils and make crippled men regain their lost power?

And these are the people who once more are rising up in rebellion against Rome?

To go at once to Rome to crush this rebellion in the bud is an instant determination. About that there can be no hesitation. Yet, suppose the rebellion be not easily crushed, what shall he do?

He has made up his mind. He will try first the art of winning them over by goodwill and generosity and humour.

In Lusius Quietus, a Moor and a creature of the uncompromising Trajan, they have had a harsh and cruel governor. He will give them one as genial as the gentlest season, a jovial governor who has no prejudices and who will let them, if they will, govern themselves.

They shall have the happy Tinnius Rufus to rule over them. They are sure to like him; and if Boadicea, who resembles a Jewess very closely, should become one, so much the better.

Should Rufus fail, then there is only one man who will not fail. If generous rule will not answer, if force, after all, must be tried, there is only one man, and there is one man, who must fill the place of Rufus and try his merciless hand.

Julius Severus must be called from Britain to Palestine, and Rufus with his Boadicea must come back to Britain.

Meantime Hadrian himself, taking with him the new governor of Palestine, must go instantly to Rome, keeping also Antinous and Tryphon, both of Jewish blood, in his councils and safe custody, loading them with honours, and using them and their wisdom to govern their own people.

With these secret resolves Hadrian and his

suite leave the camp at Londinum on their way Romewards. They pass through the people called the Cantii, rest a day or two at Durobrivæ, and then to Dubris on the southern coast, where they find a little fleet ready to carry them across to Gaul.

Their journey through Gaul, though rapid, is triumphant, for the Emperor, in order to impress the natives with his power, throws off the seclusion and privacy which are so natural to him, in order to exhibit the symbols of his authority and strength. He visits Lugdunum, the seat of the government of Gaul and the birthplace of Claudius Cæsar, and moving on to Massilia, crosses by sea to Italy, stopping only at Sardinia, and thence direct to Italy, landing at Neapolis, the ancient Parthenope, and so, by land, to Imperial Rome.

Throughout this eventful journey triumph seems to march with him every foot of the way; and yet the heart of the Emperor is low. The lowness is not without cause, for at every large centre the news of trusty and secret messengers has been of most serious import. Everywhere the report has come that the Jews are rising in great power, and with determined zeal, for the cause they live to serve. The most careful inquiry has failed to detect any proof that this resolute people possess an armoury of any kind. They have been prohibited bearing arms; they have been prohibited learning the use of arms. Where then can be the danger?

No one can answer that question, and yet every one fears. The Jews, it is whispered, have money and subtlety, and they are about to rise in rebellion.

In Sardinia they get news of the so-called rising in Cyprus. It was a scare, as it reached the ears of the Emperor, and caused Tryphon and Antinous to smile. A Roman officer had taken away by force the wife of a Jew, and the Jewesses of the place where their countrywoman was concealed, having got news of the matter, had gained entrance into the place of concealment by the stratagem of one of them, who, playing again the part of Judith, had slain the Roman offender, had let in the rest of her accomplices, had strangled all the slaves and eunuchs, and restored the stolen wife to her liberty.

Is this all? If it were, it would be foolish of a great Emperor to punish the Jews at large because a set of women resisted what every true and noble Roman would consider a foul act if it were carried out against one of his own female kindred.

The entry of the Emperor into Rome is imposing and at the same time mournful. The gate of the temple of Janus, at the foot of the capitol, is shut, in proof that universal peace reigns ; but the people are in doubt. For more than a month a comet having the shape of a sword has hung over the city ; and in the vessel which carries the Emperor from Sardinia to Neapolis one of the sacred chickens dies after communicating its fatal malady to all the rest.

Two portents of terrible meaning.

And, the day after the arrival of Cæsar it is discovered by the keeper of the temple of Janus that one of the gates of the temple is unfastened, and is moving with the wind ; a portent as potent as either of the other two.

The meeting of the Emperor and of Sabina his wife is friendly, but neither warm nor enthusiastic. They meet as old companions, glad for a moment to renew their acquaintanceship, but nothing more.

Tryphon is far more warmly welcomed, for the Empress has a favourite slave who is suffering from an issue of blood which she sets Tryphon to cure, that the sight of the blood may not longer offend her. The return of the skilled physician could not be more opportune.

Tryphon wonders how Antinous will be received by his Imperial mistress, whose will is very much law, and who knows the law as well as the will. He smooths the way for Antinous, describes his noble horsemanship, of which art the Empress is a connoisseur; expounds how the pleasant tongue, excellent spirits, and sound common sense of the youth cheer the Emperor and keep him from pursuit of false pleasures as vain reliefs from pain and languor of mind; and with the cleverest deception conveys the facts of the marvellous gifts which the youth possesses for the all but magical cure of the worst forms of human diseases.

The Empress listens at first incredulously. She will receive Antinous. She does receive Antinous, and is more incredulous still. There is something about the youth she cannot understand. Is Tryphon sure that this youth is the Antinous of Bithynia whom Pliny sent to Trajan? The parents of that youth had no repute for the possession of these divine qualities. Does he, Tryphon, believe that a youth of such low origin could possess so many virtues and accomplishments? Does the youth really possess them; or is there not in some way which she, the Empress, cannot define, though she can suspect it, a cheat or mystery going on in regard to the matter?

These are some of the Imperial woman's queries, hard to meet even by the subtlest of all the school of the Asclepiades.

One day, in confidence with Tryphon, she casts a doubt on the very sex of the popular courtier. The perplexity is at a crisis now, but gradually from this time the mind of the Empress is quieted.

Her doubts increase so much, she feels it necessary that she shall put them to the test. She must try them and prove them.

Nothing could be more fortunate for Antinous. It is one thing for a woman to doubt, it is another for her to prove a doubt of this kind.

In her early life Sabina was a famous huntress. She proposes an expedition in which Antinous shall take part. Antinous has never hunted, but has no kind of objection to take a lesson in the sport. Sabina will be to him Diana. Teaching Antinous, she will soon know by every movement, by every step of progress, what Antinous is—man, or woman in disguise. The Emperor at first demurs; he is afraid of exposing his favourite to danger, but, under a little pressure, assents, though he will not himself join in the sport; neither will Tryphon.

It is well. Sabina has the favourite entirely under her own care and observation.

They start out a goodly and handsome court to some wooded plains far away, where a boar of great and savage renown is said to be. The Empress is accompanied by quite a train of noble youths of Rome, some of whom take with them ten attendants.

Antinous takes the only attendant Antinous possesses, one who has now come to Rome to render his faithful service; Eli, the once Numidian slave of Milo the centurion, whom Fidelis bought and freed and gave away.

Eli is enraptured with the expedition; there is not one trick of skill in the hunting of the boar which he does not understand, a fact which none save Antinous knows. Between them therefore they establish a rule that in all things Antinous shall copy him, Eli ; then, soon a new and skilful hunter of hunters will be added to the field.

On their way they rest for a day in a plain, where they encamp. To pass the time they exercise themselves with bow, javelin, and spear. Antinous is the best rider of them all. Sabina grants it ; but how will he bend the bow, discharge the arrow, or throw the javelin?

Eli, ever at hand, carrying the arms, tests them first ere he places them in the hand of his master. The master, with the eye of a lynx, reads, learns, and follows every movement.

Sabina condescends to give the lesson, but Eli is the master who is followed.

No, great Empress, there is not a touch of the woman's skill in this pupil of thine! None but a youth of the male sex could ride, discharge an arrow, or cast a javelin as Antinous does it.

They reach the scene of their sport, and after another day of rest take the field. The savage animal is found and pursued. Antinous, by command of the Empress and followed by Eli, makes for a thicket on the right hand in order to intercept the animal should it turn in that direction.

The animal does not turn, and Sabina and three of her knights keep on in pursuit. In her eagerness she outstrips her followers, and soon the monster, hearing no clash of horses behind, turns round to see the solitary woman before him.

Her arrow flies and fixes itself in his side, but only with sufficient depth to enrage him the more. He approaches her in triumph, and her javelin, splendidly discharged, does worse than the arrow; it inflicts, in passing, a gaping wound on the back of the animal, and then stands obliquely fixed in the earth, buried more than half its length.

Flight is now the lonely Empress's sole resource, and grandly she takes it; but her pursuer is also grand in pursuit. Leap by leap he gains ground, and at last, seizing with his fierce jaws its heel he stops her horse with a jerk which throws her some feet forward on the ground.

She has just had time, by a side movement, to see Antinous in the distance discharging his bow. She hears the whiz of the shaft through the air, she feels the jerk that dismounts her, and she is conscious at the same time that her enemy is transfixed by the dart. She tries to raise herself to see the final struggle, and with a cry of delight as the javelin of Antinous enters the open mouth of the boar and digs itself into his heart she becomes unconscious to all further fear and all further joy.

One by one the straggling knights come up to the rescue, and, finding that their mistress lives and breathes, are ready to bear her away. Under the direction of Antinous they make a litter of their unstrung bows and cover it with mosses and soft grasses until it is turned into a springy easy couch; on this, as she afterwards remembers, a strong arm places her, an arm none less strong than that of Eli, but to her mind the arm of Antinous, and certainly not the arm of a woman.

The spoil is cut up by the knives of the

huntsmen, the head of the boar is carried on the javelin that pierced its gaping mouth, the litter bearing the Empress is borne in turn by the knights, and ere they reach the camp from which they started, the Imperial lady is so far recovered that she has but one further pang.

Acteon, her favourite hunter, torn by the boar, was so helplessly maimed that he had, for mere mercy's sake, to be slain at the spot where he fell.

But for this untoward event the return of the hunters to Rome from the chase has been a triumphal march.

The Emperor rides out in state to meet them, and Festa, the favourite slave of the Empress, follows also in the train, quite cured; cured not by Tryphon but by one his superior in deeds of cure, one who can cure *in absentia*. Festa has had a trance, during which she thought her beloved mistress had been in a danger from which she could not possibly have been saved except for Antinous, but when she recovered it was she herself who had been saved, for her malady had left her.

The voice in the trance spoke clearly the

name of Antinous ; Tryphon, usually so jealous of his own skill as a healer, admits that all the honour is due to the Emperor's favourite knight and counsellor; and the grateful Sabina, now entirely relieved of all her doubts and prejudices, joins with the rest in their praises.

Sabina has tasted, nay, has eaten her proofs, and they nourish her with so much faith in the virtues of Hadrian's favourite that she, in turn, is jealous of all other admirers of Antinous.

So in a short time the name of Antinous is a household word in Rome, and wherever else the legions going out of Rome carry Rome into the empire at large, it is a name of magical renown.

CHAPTER VIII.

LATENT WAR.

THERE are no great events in nature that are not portended.

The great cosmic convulsions of nature which occur independently of man have for their portents physical signs which men may or may not read, but which are always thrown out like the scout before the battle. The great social convulsions which come by and through man have their portents in mental phenomena. For, like the vast atmospheric sea, the mind of man in its universality has its depressions, its elevations, its storms, all of which have their portents when we are learned enough to read them.

We live for ever in a sea of mind.

The day will come when we shall know the signs which tell and foretell the perturbations the mental sea endures, its moods and tenses, it storms, its calms, its unequal measures of pulsation.

Thus it often happens before a great social convulsion that, although the social sky is clear, men feel the portents of a storm of war as they do of thunder and rain.

The portent is felt universally, the surest proof of its significance. If it travelled in lines of human intercourse it might be mere extension of rumour. When it centres in all hearts in and out of the courses of commerce and travel, it means disturbance of a sad and terrible nature.

In the period of history in which we now for a few hours assume to live, we feel and see the perturbation of the mental ocean, portending decisive war, although no new seat or cause exciting to war is definite. But the war, whenever it does break out, is to be between the all-powerful Roman and the subdued, down-trodden Jew.

Fortunatus, the friend of Servien, the Governor of Jaffa; Fortunatus, whose acquaintance we ought to cultivate more had we the time on our hands for such a true pleasure; Fortunatus, who has travelled a great deal, observed well for himself, and always taken the fate awarded to him easily ; Fortunatus smiles at the suggestion of any such portent. He asks from Servien, who shares in the general impression, for the proofs and the evidences.

'How can men who have no arms, no soldiers, no officers, and no leader, fight Rome, which is of all existences an armoury, a soldier, a general, and a Cæsar ? Absurd.'

'Their arms,' replies Lucilla, who has taken part in the debate, and who sympathises with her husband, ' their arms are their own arms, their soldiers are themselves, their general is the scholar Akiba, and their king is the King of kings and Lord of lords.'

' A woman's emotion in innocent sympathy with her own people,' responds the courtly visitor. ' I grant that if any wild enthusiasm should ever rouse them into action, if they should have amongst them a man of war who assumed to fulfil the prophecies of their Messiah, leading them to victory, then the Jews might be a thorn indeed in the side of Cæsar.'

' The point, the very point, great philosopher,' returns Lucilla.

'What every Jew believes, from Akiba to the lowest of his race, and what every Jewess believes, is that the deliverer has come.'

'But who and where is he?'

'He whom all Jews now know. The Star of Jacob, whom Akiba, directed by a star, found in the desert. He is, in our language, Bar-Cochebas, or Bar-Cohab, the son of a star. But where he is at this moment the wisest of Jews, Akiba himself, knows not. Akiba only knows that in due time, he, the ordained and pre-ordained, ordained ere ever yet the foundations of the earth were laid, will come and lead to victory the chosen people.'

The free and gentle cynicism of the gallant and happy Fortunatus was roused by the enthusiasm of Lucilla almost into a similar tone, but with a different impulse.

'A craze, a craze, noble lady; a craze of the scholar and man of the schools.' I have learned, since thou related to us the wonderful story of Akiba, something more of him than even thou knowest, and which thou shouldest add to thy narrative. Akiba is really the son of the illustrious Sisera, by one of the Jewish daughters of Jabin, king of

Tyre, whom Joseph, his reputed father, was afterwards made to marry and carry into the plains; and this child whom, led by a mirage of a Roman cavalcade, Akiba found, was the son of one of nobler blood than he.

'More about the parentage of this foundling I would not have Akiba know; for this craze of his about the youth, at present a subject of mirth were it not connected with, in all other respects, so wise and great a man, might then indeed become a serious event to Rome as well as Palestine. Happily, perchance, for him "The Son of a Star," like the wandering Pleiad, has gone forth from his constellation for ever.

'*Akiba's love put out Akiba's star!*'

'You speak in parable, good Fortunatus.'

'No parable, lady; 'tis a plain and simple matter of fact. Akiba, thou knowest, fell in love and ran away with the beautiful princess of the house of Sala, leaving the child that he had made his idol in the school of Elkanah the scribe at Cæsarea; and when he returned, as you have told us, the child and all were gone, their very house and synagogue destroyed. The story interested me so much I have been to Cæsarea and have discovered from a centurion, who played a part in it, the whole of the history.'

'And what, pray thee, is the story?'

'I will tell thee, but that which is told in the house of the Governor of Joppa must be safe as if it were in the bosom of Cæsar himself. Elkanah the scribe and teacher, fired by the enthusiasm and faith of Akiba, grew also fanatic about this mysterious youth. Setting his face against the law, he had the youth and his own daughter and only child, Huldah, taught the use of arms and horsemanship; and, finally, at a great congregation, presented the youth to the assembled people as their Messiah, Lord, and Deliverer.

'The congregation, composed of two rival communities of Jews, called respectively Samaritans and Galileans, heard the words of Elkanah with great tumult. The Galileans, of which he was one, were with him heart and soul. The Samaritans, representing an ancient feud, were opposed as heartily. The anger waxed from words to blows. With a loud and furious voice they made themselves weapons out of the wood and iron of the synagogue and of the house and school of Elkanah, and would have killed each other mercilessly but for the interposition of a tried soldier of Rome, who, coming upon the disturbers with his hundred disciplined men, surrounded them. The Jews then combined against Rome and the fight was desperate; but the Roman order and might prevailed, although a tenth of the Romans licked the dust. Every Jew who remained alive after the affray was put to death by the sword, except Elkanah, who, for a greater example, was crucified on the plain outside Cæsarea. The two children, the new Messiah of the Galilean Jews and Huldah, the daughter of Elkanah who was crucified, were found concealed in the holy place of the synagogue, and were retained until Trajan, the Emperor, should give his orders concerning them.'

'And the order was?'

'I have seen it, lady; have read it with mine own eyes. It is the most mysterious order ever penned; it is the order of a dying Emperor and soldier written and signed at the very hour of his death:

'" Let the centurion who captured the

children of the rebellious Jews take them in charge to the remotest province of the Empire. Let him teach the lad Roman arts, as if he were his own son; let the maiden be his bond-woman; and, when he dies let them be returned to my successor, with the sealed charge herewith enclosed, that the Cæsar then reigning may do with them as he seeth best. But let no Jew know whither they are exiled."

'This, lady, was the fate of the idol of Akiba, and so well has the order of Trajan been carried out, that at this moment not only no Jew, but no Roman I can find, knows the fate——'

'Of the son of Trajan,' interposed Lucilla, unable to repress her feminine skill in unravelling mysteries of birth.

'The guess may be right, lady, but it is not so set forth. It is known that there was a priestess in the temple of Daphne, near Antioch, a Jewess of the royal house of the Jewish David; that of this priestess Trajan was enamoured; that she forfeited her vows, as it is believed, for him; that, returning to her own people, she was destroyed by them; and that her sister, who as the wife of Elkanah, was also slain in the affray at Cæsarea, was a prophetess and miracle-monger named Tamar, whom Trajan knew, and in whose incantations he more than half believed.'

'Every Tamar from the first is possessed of a spirit of good or of evil; that is well known. So the children were sent forth?'

'The children were sent forth, lady, and were known in Roman and Jewish life no more. In the minds of the Jews who were allowed to remain in Cæsarea after the revolt both children were slain with the rest in the synagogue, but this strange Akiba, believing the youth to be alive, has his spies in every corner of the earth ready to deliver to him messages, in their native gibberish, by day and by night. Yet all in vain. Akiba will tire at last.'

'The Jews, good Fortunatus, have a proverb which I may repeat to thee, who lovest parables and proverbs as my Servien loves arms and horses:

"A Jew in earnest neither tires nor rests,
Till sickness wearies him or death restrains."'

'A most true proverb, my Lucilla,' broke in Servien, who had listened to the conversation in his stolid, silent manner; 'a most true proverb, as this worldly old courtier would know if he had half as many Jews to deal with as I have, without throwing in the craftiest of them all put together, that very Akiba whom both of you in your hearts so much admire, whom it is my duty to keep under vigilant eye, and never more than now, when he hath on him a fit of unusual unrest.'

While he is thus speaking a guard enters with a despatch from the Governor of Jerusalem to Servien, Governor of Joppa.

'Akiba again! There is no word but Akiba in all the Jewish mouths. The word will be found engraven on my heart should I ever be sold to the disciples of Eristratus, who cut up men alive, to see the movements of life. I would to Jupiter that Akiba had never come out of Paradise, or that he would go back to it for good. Vale! vale!'

And so saying, as he read the despatch from Jerusalem, the faithful and worried Governor of Joppa, good and honest soldier, but no match for untiring genius fanned by the spirit of liberty, leaves his companions.

To each quarter of Joppa the Roman

governor bends his steps, to see with his own eyes that every man under him is at his post. He has about him no guard, for he wishes to be alone, to see and judge for himself. Besides, his sentinels are all within call, and these Jews, troublesome as they may be, are so utterly helpless they can do him no possible physical injury.

He is musing to himself, as he goes slowly along, after the manner of a man who will resume a conversation or a controversy when next he rejoins his family circle. He is wondering, in his way, as to what these Jews can possibly want beyond what they have. They enjoy, he reasons, all the advantages of Roman rule; they have really the same liberty as the noblest Roman subject. Some of them are Jews of the old schools, some are philosophers; some belong to one or other of the sects called Essenes, Nazarenes, Gnostics, Ebionites: and every one of these people is allowed to exercise his own religious rites, even though he empties the temples of the Roman gods and almost stops the demand for the sacrifices. Moreover, they can buy and sell, amass money, plant vineyards, marry and be given in marriage, travel wherever they please, write histories, cultivate music and science; do, in fact, everything except rule and govern.

'What more can they want? They say they want liberty, so that they shall not be the servants of Cæsar. But what liberty has Servien which every Jew has not? Is not Servien also a servant of Cæsar? Why, his own name carries the fact, and his own duty, servitude of servitudes, confirms it. Side by side with him this man Akiba is a king to a slave.'

Servien is at heart as just and gentle a man as a Roman soldier can be, but he revolts up to the point of the worst cruelty against the men and women who are so obstinate and rebellious towards Roman rule and their own good.

Should any one tell Servien that liberty does not mean mere permission to enjoy what a conquering race in its generosity or, may be, its policy permits to a conquered race; should any wise and far-seeing man tell Servien that this question of liberty is entirely a racial question, and that a Jew can no more conform to Roman rule than a Roman could conform to Jewish; did any one show to Servien that if he, Servien and all his brethren, were under the dominion of Akiba as the Jewish Emperor of the world, he and they would be precisely what he and they now detest, men everlastingly plotting to free themselves from the dominion that is held over them, he would not listen to such arguments; they would be too impractical and too absurd.

'Nonsense,' he would say, 'these people I am set to govern are false, by nature, to all except themselves. They are, by the side of us rulers, a degraded set, dissatisfied with Cæsar and with everything. Coerce them, coax them as much as you may, they are still ready to rise if you take off an ounce weight of the required repression. Give them their wish to govern themselves, and they will merely quarrel amongst themselves and invite us to rule them again. They are not capable of self-government; and shall we dismember the empire of the world to please some five millions of such a race? Ridiculous idea! Let Rome and Cæsar reign for ever. By means fair or foul Rome has accepted the trust of governing these people, and she were a coward now, out of a mere sentiment, to give up the trust. To the conquered as well as the conqueror it were unfair to the loyal section of the conquered to give up one poor pennyweight of authority. Let Rome give just laws and enforce their obedience, and let Rome and Cæsar live for ever.'

He has arrived just so far in his meditations when his attention is diverted by an entirely new phenomenon.

He has reached a point near to one of the schools under the charge of Akiba, from which a tower abuts that has been built for astronomical purposes. Fortunatus and himself have more than once visited that tower, to notice the very curious observations of the movements of the heavenly bodies that are being made from it. An ingenious artisan from Alexandria has put up a glass by which the images of the moon and stars are cast on the floor of the tower by night, the disc of the sun by day. He has placed figures on this floor in a circle, and the sun, moon, and stars seem to traverse the circle, through more or less of its circumference, according to the seasons. To mark these courses lines have been drawn on the floor of the tower, and these, reduced in size, have been copied by the students into maps or charts of the heavenly bodies in their daily or nightly rounds.

Fortunatus says it is the most wonderful instrument that has been made since the days of Heraclitus, and Akiba is pleased with it, but rather in a tone of secondary quality, which is peculiar in him.

'Perhaps,' Servien suggests, ' because he is jealous of the inventor.'

' Akiba knows no such passion as jealousy, my old Servien. If he did, he were dead long ere this. Jealousy is a certain poison if it affect even the noblest minds. You have no arrow so swift, no javelin so sure. Akiba is not jealous, that is certain, but he also is not really interested, which is indeed singular. It is in my mind that the invention is for service rather than for curiosity or learning, and that this tower conceals some other uses or intentions.'

So reasons the worldly Fortunatus on the last visit he and Servien have paid to the tower; and now Servien, all alone and thinking of other things, is within sight, so far as the light of the brilliant stars will permit, of this curious structure.

He raises his eyes to look at it, lying in dull shadow from the other buildings, when suddenly there seems to shoot from it a ball, like a stone thrown from a catapult.

The missile, whatever it may be, falls with tremendous force one stride from his feet.

Undoubtedly Servien, the Governor of Joppa, was a moment ago only one step from death.

A Roman governor is not a man to fear and, instantly, this one stoops to pick up the missile. It is broken by the fall into twenty pieces of sharp hard substance like crystal, and it has scattered round it a quantity of dust, which, as Servien accidentally stirs it, bursts into yellow flame that spreads wherever the powder has spread and gives out an odour like garlic, but much sharper and more oppressive.

Happily, as he afterwards thinks, a rather sharp wind is blowing away the vapour which rises from this damnable fire, or he might now be killed by the fumes of it. The fire soon dies out; it has sufficed by its light to enable the undismayed governor to pick up the fragments of crystal, and all is over.

The fragments of crystal must be reserved for Fortunatus to see and examine; so Servien, soldierlike, utilises his metal helmet for carrying them. The helmet has served him before now for a vessel holding water, and more than once for holding small articles of spoil, so it is ready to his hand.

Carrying the fragments he has picked up, he retraces his steps to a guard-house he has just left, and in a safe place conceals them there under lock and key, without one soul seeing him.

The interval gives him time to reflect on what shall next be done. Did he follow his own pure soldierlike impulse he would call out a guard and at once, by force, suddenly enter the tower of observation and pull it down to the ground. But, what would Fortunatus say to this? Would he not call it a rash and unstatesmanlike act, the very act to raise a tumult and ensure a foolish failure? Fortunatus is a mile away from Servien, and no time should be lost in this inquiry. Servien must do something. What shall he do?

A mere trifle is apt to lead to a decision in circumstances like these. On the sea he observes, as he leaves the guard-house, a thin streak of light reflected from a window in the gable of a part of the schools standing on the shore. It is the reflection of the light from the study of Akiba. Akiba, then, is still at his studies. He will visit Akiba off his guard. It will be quite natural for him, Servien, on his rounds to wish to see the floor of the tower at midnight, when the stars are chronicling their courses, and, there being a light in the window of the philosopher, he need not hesitate to solicit the favour. As governor he has the right to go wherever he may list at any time, but he will put it as a favour, so as to conceal all suspicion of alarm.

With perfectly collected soldierly manner Servien carries out his project. He passes with measured tread under the window of the student; he opens the door of the vestibule or passage leading to the door of the study; not a door is barred, and all is as quiet as a sepulchre. An immense staircase, leading up to the schools, is darker than the sky outside and quite as solemnly noiseless and vacant.

He enters the study or sanctum of the scholar with a kind of awe creeping over him, which is an entirely new sensation. It is a sensation made up partly of dislike to be, as a soldier, engaged in a secret service, an espial, the work of a mean man paid for a useful, perhaps, but ignoble service. It is a sensation also of some mysterious fear of this wonderful man who has entered, as Lucilla believes, the Paradise of the Jews and has come out alive.

To these feelings may be added that sense of diffidence or difficulty which always comes on a person who is about for the first time to speak to a great and remarkable man with whom alone he has never exchanged a word.

These combined feelings so influence Servien that, if there had been time, he might have given up his design at the last moment. This is impossible, for as he enters the sanctum the dark eyes of Akiba are shining lustrously upon him. Akiba is seated in a recess immediately in front of the door, the light of a lamp on his left hand enabling him to see from his obscurity every thing and every movement in the room, whilst it reflects himself dimly, almost terribly. He is at his writing-table with all his books about him, the stylus in his hand and the parchment or paper he is inscribing upon, from right to left, under his hand.

As Servien enters Akiba rises, and doffing his berretta and adjusting his silken robe over his shoulders, bows to his unexpected visitor with a calm and dignified expression that is more effective than any spoken welcome.

Servien in turn is moved to ceremony: he raises his metal cap with his right hand, rests his left hand on the hilt of his sword, and bends down his honest head as if he were about to ask a blessing from the Rabbi before him.

'Salve, salve, noble Servien!' is the greeting of Akiba; ''tis indeed an honour for a poor scholar of a despised race to receive by night a visit from the Vice-Cæsar of Joppa. Is it for any service my learning or skill can render my lord and governor?'

'I know it to be an unearthly hour to call on the renowned Akiba,' returns Servien, 'but a man walking in the night grows weary of monotony, and seeing thy light burning, I was drawn, as it were, to court thee in order to ask a favour.'

'To us scholars, my lord, time is no clement. We are children of time and live in its essence. It is our father and our destroyer; it feeds us and kills us; it lifts us into fame and it carries us into oblivion.'

'A bright fame and a far-distant oblivion for Akiba!'

'Nay, illustrious friend, if I may so call a truly brave and honest soldier, fame is fleeting and oblivion is sure. But what, I pray thee, is it I can do for thee?'

'A simple favour indeed. Some days since my old comrade and visitor, the courtly Fortunatus, a bosom friend of Cæsar, went with me to the roof of the tower thou hast built, on which the Alexandrian inventor has made the heavenly bodies trace their own records. We saw the record done in the day, and the lustre of the stars led me to wish to see the same by night.'

'Is that all the Governor of Joppa requires?' replies Akiba. 'Then, indeed, it is a small favour. Let us go at once.'

And, placing a white precious stone, pure

as snow, on his parchments to keep them in their place, and arranging the books in order with silken marks, the great scholar takes up his midnight lamp and gracefully leads the way.

The two men ascend the grand staircase to the top by four flights ; they turn to the left hand sharply at the top, and traversing a long corridor on each side of which, with open doors, some hundred Jewish youths are sleeping the deep sleep of innocence, if faces are indices of human nature, they pass on to the floor of the tower, leaving the lamp of Akiba in a deep recess in the wall of the corridor made to receive a lamp or candle.

On the tower not a breath is heard nor sound of any kind, save what they themselves make, but the sight before them is splendid. The white circle around the floor of the tower stands out luminously, and within two dark lines or girdles upon it the stars above are reflected, the condensing apparatus moving, as it seems, with them by means of a weight which descends from the tower to the earth.

'And pray thee, great scholar,' asks Servien,

as he surveys the curious sight, ' of what use is this business when it is fulfilled ? '

'Ah! there, my lord, thou puzzlest me. It is to my mind more curious than useful, but the ingenious contriver, being one of our own people from Alexandria, came to me with the design, bearing a letter of such strong recommendation that I let him have his way, as a pleasure to himself and an amusement to the schools. For my own part, I have looked upon it as more fitted for a follower of Aristotle than of Moses, and to-morrow it is ordered to be removed, lest it lead the youth of this place from the worship of the Father of Light and Creator of all things to that of Baal or Apollo. I have seen its evil tendencies. This very day that is just past two scholars, debating about it, were so misled as to surmise that the sun, the moon, and the stars were not made for the special purposes of this great earth, and quoted the lines of Virgil, one of your own writers, who most profanely teaches that the earth, a mere ball like the moon, floats in the firmament, and, by its own motion round the fixed sun, makes the seasons for itself.'

'Virgil, I have heard, was a poet of the

time of Augustus Cæsar, and we all know what poets are when they get on the wing: they live by writing what could never take place; if they didn't they wouldn't be poets,' returned the matter-of-fact governor.

Then pausing for a moment he added:

'Nevertheless, I am glad this tower is coming down; it is bad to have anything that creates innovation and unsettles the sensitive minds of the impressionable young. I argue that thou art right; but this inventor, what of him when his skill is no more required? He might be of service to Rome, and certainly would vastly please Fortunatus. Let him come to me to-morrow in the first hours, and we will find him business which shall be mutually advantageous. Hadrian himself would extend his patronage to one so skilful.'

'It is a thought worthy the Governor of Joppa, and I will deliver it to the young Archimedes, who is so much honoured, should he ever return. But he is gone. Thinking he might be hurt at seeing his much-admired folly destroyed, I let him sail back to Alexandria to work at some new invention he has there, which to thee, as a soldier, might be precious, but which to my scholars will not be so desirable, seeing that it has to do with the burning of fleets, the storming of great cities, and other arts of war intended for the slaughter, as opposed to the protection, of mankind.'

'Is it,' asked Servien, rather too eagerly to escape the watchful gaze of Akiba, who, with his lamp again in his hand, is showing his visitor back through the corridor—'is it something that is projected from a catapult and that bursts into flame when it strikes the object at which it is directed?'

'Something of that nature, I believe,' replied Akiba in so frank and open a voice as to entirely remove all kind of hasty suspicion in which Servien might have indulged ; 'a kind of improved Greek fire, cast, not by a catapult, but by some spring or impulse derived from itself when set on fire by the will of the owner of the vile thing. Will my lord not honour me by taking a few moments' rest in my room of books ere he departs for the night?'

The invitation comes quite naturally just as they return to the door of Akiba's study, and Servien, intensely interested in what he has heard, is nothing loath to re-enter.

Akiba presents him with dried figs, bread and pure water, of which, for courtesy's sake, he partakes in moderate degree. His taste at this moment is for knowledge rather than for figs and water.

Raising the lamp to the walls, and leading his visitor round the room, the great Rabbi exhibits to him some of his choicest written treasures of Hebrew learning. 'These, my lord, are the dead that never die, the friends that never quarrel, the foes that are never extinguished, the slumbering fires from which men thousands upon thousands of years hence will light their torches, charged with new fuel, and go forth with into the world, spreading knowledge until all men shall know all things. Then shall come the end foretold by our glorious seer, "When knowledge shall cover the earth as the waters cover the sea."'

There is something in the fire of expression, the depth of feeling, the command of thought, conveyed by the words thus uttered that makes even the slow heart of the Roman governor beat high within him. He feels a pulsation in his throat, and, convinced that, if he stays longer with the master of men in whose hands he now is, he shall betray some weakness, he thanks his host most warmly and, like a prudent general, beats a hasty retreat back to his own quarters and the beloved Lucilla.

'No wonder,' he says to himself as he resumes his musing, 'no wonder that this man rules youths and women and impressionable men in the way he does, when he has made me, a soldier and governor, feel such a strange and inward glow. A moment more and I had given way to my emotions.'

And the more he feels the truth springing from this contemplation the faster he walks, until the physical effort catches up the mental and, sustaining the rapid action of the heart by its ruder influence, leaves the mind once more free to pursue its own sober course.

The resumption of his ordinary mental faculties is not altogether so satisfactory to Servien as he could wish. He has gained some useful facts, he has missed some important facts, and he has lost in decision of purpose. On the whole he is a loser. Most singular truth of all, he, the cautious soldier, is impressed, in spite of all he has seen, with a sensation he cannot throw off, that he is at war with the mysterious scholar he has just left in so friendly a manner. The fall of that fireball from the school of Akiba is the first act of defiant rebellion. It means war and a clean sweep of Roman power if the whole of the Jews be not driven into the sea once more.

One point is quite certain: the ball of fire which fell at his feet was the work of the youth whom Akiba had sent back to Alexandria. Fortunatus must be sent off there to inquire after that youth, and the schools of Joppa must be watched with more care than ever. Some one of those sleeping dogs has, no doubt, got the secret of the Greek fire and projectile force, and, unknown to the master, is practising the use of the weapon. If one student has only one such instrument in his possession, each student may in a short time have the same, and a few thousands of these may suffice in an hour to burn out the whole Roman legion of Joppa.

With these thoughts Servien seeks his repose. He is a strong man, because he is a strong and sound sleeper, and having been up late he sleeps late, so much later by far than he has intended that, when he moves from his chamber to enjoy the luxury of his bath, he finds the lively Fortunatus bathed, breakfasted, and equipped for the day.

In a few words Servien relates to his astonished friend the events of the night.

'We must see that tower again before it is dismantled,' is the first observation of Fortunatus as he ceases to hear the story. 'Let me fetch thee thy stylus and parchment, that thou mayest write to Akiba at once.'

The materials brought, the friends indite and send the following letter:—

SERVIEN, GOVERNOR OF JOPPA, TO AKIBA, THE CHIEF RABBI OF THE JEWS, GREETING.

Servien would wish to revisit the tower before it is demolished, in order that his friend Fortunatus may observe with him the procession of the heavenly bodies by night.

Ave Cæsar!

'The missile which fell at thy feet, my Servien,' continued Fortunatus after a short time given to reflection, 'was cast by a human hand which did not calculate for the adverse force of the wind. It was cast also by a tall man, who could reach over the wall or battlement of the tower. When we are on the tower I will indicate to thee where and how it was done.'

'That thou wilt never do,' returns Servien as he peruses the reply which the messenger has quickly brought. 'Hear thou this :—

AKIBA, SUBJECT OF CÆSAR, TO SERVIEN, GOVERNOR OF JOPPA, WITH AKIBA'S HOMAGE.

The request of the noble Servien comes, unfortunately, too late. The tower, invaded by five hundred friendly enemies, was destroyed at sunrise, in compliance with the command issued to the schools at sunset, yesterday ; and all the delicate mechanical instruments have been committed to the furnace for more useful after-application.

AKIBA.

With a light laugh Fortunatus takes the document from the hand of the Governor of Joppa, reads it for himself, and lays it down with the remark :

'Latent war! latent war! my friend of friends, and the first cast with the learned Jew.'

CHAPTER IX.

IN LIGHT AND IN SHADOW.

Leviathan with its happy, now twice happy pair, carries its occupants across the western sea to a country and temporary home which to Simeon is a new world of beauty and splendour, such as he has never dreamed of or conceived possible.

From the first he is affected by his environments, and the influence of these so increases as the days and months roll on that at last he becomes, in the strictest sense of the word, a new creature. His tastes have changed; his ideas of men and events and things have changed; the past is to him a something he has buried, and which does not any longer belong to him. For an interval the present is his only life.

In the midst of it all one leading idea is,

nevertheless, fixed firmly in his mind and heart, the belief in his own destiny. He is born not for himself alone; not to live and work and play and marry and have children and grow old and die as others do, but to perform some pre-ordained task, fulfil some great purpose which has been predicted of him by wise and inspired men who have been dead ages before he was born.

Simeon had received this idea of his own importance, in the first instance, from those by whom he was surrounded in the earliest days of his conscious life.

He had imbibed it as the food of his soul, on which his soul was nourished from its earliest mouldings in the vesture of clay which it occupied. The vesture has adapted itself in its growth and development to the thought or idea, and the abstract has become the concrete. The idea, moreover, is fed by other forces. There is in Simeon an unhesitating taint and touch of pride, an unflinching courage, and a stubbornness which nothing can appal, nothing can subdue; and, underlying all these, is the genius of superstition respecting divine purposes and mysteries which would have fitted him for the service of the temple, had he been called to it, independently of the arts which embellish that service and give to it human understanding.

In spite of all this, the still flexible and impressionable nature of the man might yet, perhaps, be diverted, did the philosopher Leon and the adorable Erine lend their minds and words and acts to the task of leading him from his past life exclusively to theirs, for with them he is already great amongst the great. He is accepted as the affianced of the maiden of love of the island of Peace and Beauty in which his happy lines are now cast, and he finds, in the island, details of pleasure and duty amply sufficient to satisfy a mind far more capacious and able than his own.

Strangely, both Leon and Leon's daughter are infected with the same idea as Simeon's earlier friends. They, too, believe that he is predestined to some great and mighty future.

Leon the scholar and interpreter has read it on the breast of his protégé; Erine has learned from her father the writing and its meaning, and sharing with him in all his thoughts, and believing in all his knowledge, has accepted the fate of her lover with his heart, and in the boundlessness of her love has given her own heart to his fate as well as to him.

Thus the ideal of the grand destiny is fanned rather than subdued in the soul of Simeon.

He has gone through great perils: he has been saved by miraculous interpositions: Leon and Erine have been instruments by and through which he has been saved. Why?

The answer comes to them all alike.

'That he may perform the task for which he is sent into the world.'

Ah, sweet child, divine Erine Leoline, well mayst thou feel that thine heart is divided between two loves; love of him who is thine heart's choice; love of the mighty service which it is thy lover's allotted duty to perform.

Doth thy cheek suddenly grow pale when the blush of pure love has tinted it but a moment before; doth the blush retreat back to thy heart?

So must it be. But, cheer thee up, dear maiden: should he be called even to leave thee, the greater will be the joy when he returns to thy beloved arms, his great task accomplished, and a world saved from slavery and sin by his puissant might and majesty.

These are cross thoughts; the one bitter as death, the other bright as everlasting glory. Thoughts that will well up even though they quiet down with the thankful recognition of the present fact. 'As yet he is here, and is mine in the golden chains of never-ending love.'

The place where these devoted lovers now live is of itself a natural home of love and beauty.

It is called Juverna, the island of eternal youth. Once from the mysterious East there came a fleet of strangers in boats or galleys of oak and gold with sails white as the wings of a dove. The strangers landed, and, struck with the beauty of the country, planted themselves as exiles who had alighted in the very home they sought for. They found in possession of the island a small, weak, and yet savage race, whom they at first drove inland, but soon won to themselves by the exercise of a combined religion and art so pure that it attached all things to itself.

The chief of this friendly enemy carried

the figure of a lion on his standard, and from him descended a line of successors of whom our Leon the wise is the last and not the least. They were not kings either by name or by office, for from the first the government had been after the manner of a republic, in which the virtues reigned alone. But the family that bore the lion as the type of its dignity and strength in the old Milesia, from whence originally came all the families, has retained its pre-eminence from father to son through many generations.

Now for the first time the continuity of the male line is broken, to the overwhelming grief of all the island; but in time, as the grief has healed, the presence of the beautiful and motherless daughter of Leon begins to raise the exceeding sorrow into equal joy. The loveliness, the sweetness, the gentleness of this child of the chief of this lovable people are traits soon known everywhere, so that she, Erine Leoline, becomes as an angel amongst her race, her name sacred as the good spirit of Juverna. The gentle Erine, the Maiden of Love!

Of this beloved child stories and poems

are written, intended to pass down to the latest day of time. Timæus of Elbana, in Juverna, Timæus bard of bards, travelling, like blind Homer, from town to town, is never tired of singing her virtues, and never wearies his listeners when she is the theme of his inspiration.

'Sing us, good Timæus,' the children and young folks say, 'sing us once more "The Maiden of Love."'

And as they form a ring round him the older folk fall in and listen and applaud as eagerly as the young.

Then Timæus, full of his song, touches his harp as if it were a spirit as he sings:

The Maiden of Love.

Erine Leoline, whenever thy shadow
    Falls on the earth as the sun falls on thee,
Mountain and mountain stream, river and meadow,
    Sing forth thy praises to nature and me.

' Come,' cries the mountain, ' sweet Erine, and press,
    Press with thy feet my rugged old side:
Ascend to my summit, that mountains may guess
    When thou art my crown how great is my pride.'

' Come,' cries the mountain stream, ' come to me, dearest,
    Drink with thy lips the kisses I throw.
Kisses of spray and crystals the clearest,
    Bright as the sunbeam and pure as the snow.'

'Come,' cries the river, 'oh come to my breast,
　That I may convey thee on torrent and tide :
So the waters of life which I bear shall be blest
　As the bridegroom is blest when he bears off his bride.'

'Come,' cries the meadow in mantle of flowers,
　Buttercups, daisies, and cowslips galore ;
'Come, and the kine, in the shades of my bowers,
　Shall sport with their young as they ne'er did before.'

'Come,' cries the bard, ' sweet light of the skies,
　Light that concealeth the mansions above !
Come for a moment, illumine these eyes,
　That my soul may behold the maiden of love.

'Then, tho' my harp-strings were flaccid and dumb ;
　Then, tho' my voice could no music retain :
Then, tho' my heart were silent and numb,
　My life would return and with it my strain.'

Throughout all Juverna Erine Leoline the beloved wanders, fearing no evil. For here there is neither wealth nor poverty, to make men sinful. Wealth makes no poverty; poverty makes no wealth.

To Simeon, nurtured, ever since he left the shepherd's cot, in the sight of teeming wealth and imperial power by the side of starving want and abject feebleness, the government and condition of this noble people of Juverna are at once a lesson and a marvel.

It is not altogether new to him in theory, for he has gathered it in prophecy; it is like the Zion which he has heard foretold, but which as yet his eye has not seen until now. Surely he, the child of destiny, has been specially sent here to learn the wisdom and the practice that shall make glorious his own reign, when it comes, the reign of Zion, even as Zion has been depicted and foretold.

To Erine he would sometimes speak of this hope in terms which she at once idolises and reproves.

'True, my own, there is no one more fitted to reign over all the world than thou art, but why shouldst thou reign? Why in thy great and universal kingdom should not all be kings and no man more than another, just as here, and as we who have faith in the life eternal believe it will be hereafter?'

'Because, dear Erine, the prophecy conveys that a king shall rule in righteousness, and all the world shall fear him.'

'I like not "rule," I like not "fear," my Simeon. They are harsh words, even out of the mouth of one of thy prophets. I would have all rule by love, not fear. If I feared thee, I, even I, should not love thee. Why, then, should the people whom thou art destined to save?'

'We will divide the difference. Thou, Erine, will be queen of my kingdom, and thou shalt win by love while I will rule by fear, so shall both the bold and the cowardly be equally under governance, and the nobler part thy subjects.'

'Unfair, unjust, Simeon to give to me the best and keep the worst thyself. No, we must have no subjects, no mastering human power, no fear, but all equal; equal faith, equal fraternity, equal fidelity, equal favour, equal freedom, equal frankness, equal friendship; the seven great virtues all equally distributed and practised.'

'But, my dreaming angel, will that meet the prophecy?'

'Entirely. The king of the prophecy is not a human being like unto thee. Thou art the servant of the king who shall reign. The king himself is the "Ra," the "Yes," the "I am," the "Existence" whose kingdom hath no beginning and no end. Of him our sacred scriptures also speak, and he it is who must reign. Thou mayest guide, we may guide if I may share the dangers as well as the glories with thee, but He must reign.'

'What Erine says is Simeon's will.'

'Tis thus that Simeon is loved, and reasoned with, and hoped for, and trusted; his strong unyielding nature, if an opposing enemy lies in the way, bending with the suppleness of a willow bough to the gentle breath of his angelic guide and stay.

CHAPTER X.

ROMAN AND JEW.

The Court of Hadrian at Rome was never so peculiar as it is now that the Emperor has returned with Antinous the new courtier.

'What is there about Antinous that Cæsar should so worship Antinous? The parents of Antinous, were they not Bithynians of poor means and position? Was not Antinous himself the freed slave of the younger Pliny, when that great philosopher was Governor of Bithynia, and made by him a present to Trajan, who left him to Hadrian with the rest of the imperial chattels? Why, then, should Antinous be the worshipped of Cæsar?' So all the creatures of the Court inquire.

For by this time the admiration of Hadrian for the favoured knight of Rome has become to all, except Tryphon, who knows the whole secret, a mystery. Antinous is the very genius of Hadrian, is consulted on every project, every whim; and is held up as being more than mortal, as a possessor of divine powers, as a healer and miracle-worker, nay, as little less than a deity.

Sabina the Empress to some extent shares in the admiration.

Perhaps she finds Hadrian more easily pleased and, if such a term be allowable towards so magnificent a spouse, more manageable through the medium of Antinous than if no such power were present. Perhaps the Empress herself is won by the courtly manners and gifts of the handsome knight, who is so discreet, wise, and skilful.

'Why does Tryphon, the physician, follow in the same course of admiration? He once had first place with Cæsar. Why does he resign it?'

The courtiers ask this question also, and one of them, bolder than the rest, puts it to Tryphon direct, to receive the candid answer:

'Because Antinous has diviner gifts, and uses them wisely.'

Tinnius Rufus is in due course installed Governor of Palestine, and with Boadicea takes up his residence in Jerusalem, where he is soon in a sea of trouble with his subjects. In his good-natured fashion he tries to bring Jew and Roman into terms of good friendship. At a vast expense he prepares a banquet of the richest kind, to which he invites the leaders of both peoples. The Jewish leaders come, because they dare not do otherwise. They take their places, and are well pleased to see that they are put on an equality with their rulers, but not one of the good things which the hospitable Rufus has put before them will they touch with their lips. They dare not eat of food that is unclean.

The Romans make up for the Jewish abstinence. The Romans eat, drink, and are merry; but when they are inflamed with wine they lose their serenity and forget their good manners. They talk to themselves apart, and they do not altogether conceal the wish that the task were permitted them of thrusting the good viands down the throats of their obstinate visitors with the points of their swords.

Rufus, as host, does all he can, according to his nature, to conciliate both parties. He calls for the musicians, who sing exquisitely and play their instruments of music. He tries the dancers. It is all in vain. The Romans exult; the Jews are decorously subdued and silent. It is his duty to declare the health of Cæsar. The Romans rave in applause and raise their wine-cups above their heads, and dash the wine down their throats and shout 'Ave Cæsar!' until they are hoarse. The Jews rise solemnly and say something, which in the confusion no Roman can understand. It is fortunate. In the expressive language of their tongue, and in the language of their hearts, they have cursed Cæsar as sincerely as the Romans have hailed him.

The banquet is an acknowledged failure.

Not disheartened, Rufus, who is as patient as he is honest and good-tempered, determines to make a journey through all parts of his province. He sends the suggestion to Hadrian, and Hadrian returns his hearty approval. 'It is what he, the Emperor, would do were he the Governor of Palestine.'

Rufus makes his journey, accompanied by the indomitable Boadicea.

Proceeding northwards on the eastern side of the province he visits Scythopolis, the most famous of military stations, and onwards from there to Cæsarea Philippi. Returning southward by the Sea of Galilee, he bends south-westerly to Cæsarea on the coast of the Great Sea. Here he stays for a few days, inspecting the coast, studying the fortifications, and reviewing the troops which lie in the encampments.

The journey for the greater part of it is not a success. It fails, like the banquet. To the name of Cæsar the Jews pay their homage, and no charge can be brought against any Jew, be he of the old Mosaic school, an Ebionite, an Essene, a Gnostic, or a Nazarene. But between himself and the Jews, and between the Romans generally and the Jews, Rufus can establish no bond of union whatsoever.

It surprises him most to find, above all things unexpected, that Boadicea is by far the greatest favourite of all his Court.

Boadicea has assumed the princess, and she carries it well. Boadicea, like the Jews, belongs to a race that is being held down by Roman power.

Boadicea in her heart hates the Romans; and although there may not be a Jew in all

Palestine who knows a word of her or of her race, the similar position of her race and theirs creates a spontaneous sympathy in her which is reciprocated so fully that even the unsuspecting Rufus observes it, and, to tell the truth, utilises it as the one and only good thing which the virago ever did to make him contented with his lot. Dressed in the costume of a lady of Rome and wife of the Governor of a Roman province, Boadicea is a woman of mark. Her eyes are a deep blue, her hair an intense black, a combination at once rare and fascinating. Her features are noble, her expression is commanding, and sometimes, as she tames down by mixing with new and agreeable society, dignified.

In the Roman community her fame as a virago has run before her, and caused her to be looked upon with some alarm; but to the Jews all this is concealed, and from the very circumstance that she is obviously different to the Romans, she is the better appreciated.

To the Jews she is affable, and, as far as lies in her nature, kind; it must also be added to her credit that, while she admires her husband none the more nor despises him none the less because he is the governor of a province, she seizes every opportunity of conciliating those under him, whoever they may be, to his authority.

If Simeon the brave Jew, who defied Cæsar in Britain; if the Numidian bear, who fought the wolves; or, if the gallant Antinous had been the lord and master of Boadicea, she were an excellent wife; so she feels and so she informs the unhappy Rufus every time when they hold any altercation, which is about once a day at least.

From Cæsarea on the Great Sea they travel to Joppa, where Servien is still in power, and where he and Lucilla play the host and hostess to their superior in command with becoming grace.

Fortunatus has long left Joppa, failing entirely to open the eyes of Servien to any real danger from the schools of Akiba. The incident of the casting of the fireball is out of mind, and, except that more students than ever press into and pass out of the schools, things are little changed.

Yet just at this moment a change ought to

be forcing itself on the notice even of trustful and dull Servien. The Jewish youths are bolder than they were of yore; they are proud of their superior knowledge, and, like all acute minds in the medium stage between knowledge and wisdom, they are proud of the subtlety which passes for wisdom. Amongst themselves they openly commend the cultivation of every subtle art, whatever may be the cost of self-respect and strict honour through which it is obtained; and, despite all his other grand qualities, their master, the renowned head of the schools, does not rebuke them for what they do. He himself will be wise whenever he can; when he cannot be wise he also will be subtle.

One of these students, returning from Alexandria, has gathered there the calculation of an eclipse of the sun on a date and at an hour perfectly foretold. The fact is communicated to Akiba, who holds it, for the subtlest of purposes, to be used if ever required.

The pursuit of subtlety gives birth to a pride which cannot long be concealed. It is evidenced in every town and village of

Palestine into which the scholars are dispersed as they leave Joppa.

Fortunatus writes to Servien, from Scythopolis, a letter, which arrives during the visit of Rufus.

FORTUNATUS TO SERVIEN, GOVERNOR OF JOPPA.

The subtlety of Akiba is everywhere; the fountain of it in Joppa and under thine own nose. If thou smell it not, thou art duller than Cerberus, who grew duller as his heads were multiplied. There is no such man as Akiba in all the world. I have apprised Cæsar of him, and even he will not believe, so I can forgive thee; but for all that I pray of thee beware.

FORTUNATUS.

'I should think Fortunatus might be right if he had convinced Cæsar,' is the remark of Servien as he communicates the letter to Rufus.

An incident, which would be considered really droll if it were not connected with a subject of the most solemn import, springs out of the warning which Servien has communicated to the Governor of Palestine.

The Governor, in making it, has confided to his virago the history of Akiba. The virago has listened with the keenest admiration. Simeon, the Numidian, Antinous are splendid men, but, now, to Akiba they are mere foils. She assumes that she has fallen in love with the great man, whom she has never known except through the terms in which her husband and others have spoken of him. She makes no concealment of her sincere madness on this point.

One day she asks : ' Has Akiba a wife ? '

Lucilla tells to Boadicea the story of Akiba's first love, of the death of that first love, and of his continuous and faithful widowhood.

The admiration of the virago intensifies to rapture. There is no man living like Akiba.

The enthusiasm of his wife puts a new idea into the mind of Rufus, which idea, as his most intimate friends know, is fanned by another, warmer and even more persuasive one, in the way of a little counter love passion of his own which he has contracted for a Tyrian damsel who has danced before him at Cæsarea on the Great Sea.

It is a very odd thing that a fat Roman governor, who has passed the meridian of life, should be stricken with such a counter-passion; but so it is, and the Tyrian dancer would make him dance the fool with her to her heart's content if Boadicea were not in the way.

Boadicea is in the way, and that in a manner unmistakable. Up to this time she has never had occasion to be jealous of any other woman. What she would be if she became jealous is too fearful to be contemplated. The mere thought of it keeps Rufus from the sleep he loves even more than a woman.

At last, after profoundest study and many dinners unusually sumptuous, Rufus makes up his resolve.

He will offer his own Boadicea as a present to Akiba and then at once return to Jerusalem.

Everything commends this plan to his mind. Boadicea, still handsome and, when she likes, winsome, admires Akiba to madness. Akiba, after all, is but a man, and is certainly as likely to be entranced by Boadicea as he, Rufus, was when he first knew her. It will show great friendship on his, Rufus's, part to the illustrious Jew; great self-sacrifice; and, best of all—Rufus chuckles over this until his fat sides ache to each other—it will take a thorn out of those sides and put one into the sides of Akiba that will torment his cleverest contemplations and spoil the most skilful plans which his shrewd genius ever laid out.

To win Akiba to his scheme Rufus treats him with a respect like that of a child to a father. He visits the scholar daily at the schools and comes, like every one else, under the spell of the fascinator.

One day in sly jest Akiba tells him: 'Smoke did not rise from the tomb of thy father.'

It is a Jewish proverb, meaning that the father of Rufus had not left behind him in his representative so much as a column of smoke.

It had happened that the pyre on which the father of Rufus was consumed, having been made of dry and light material, blazed in a sharp wind so briskly that it actually gave forth no smoke.

Therefore, on hearing the observation of Akiba, Rufus, accepting the statement in its literal sense, as a declaration conveying a fact which Akiba could not have heard by any ordinary channel of human communication, inquires, 'By what art of divination didst thou, most extraordinary man, know a fact known only to myself?'

'It is the genius of my race to know all things under the sun,' responds Akiba.

With this subtle answer Rufus is still more mysteriously confounded, while Boadicea, who is present, makes no concealment of the joy she feels at her husband's stupidity and Akiba's wisdom.

As if to second her husband's clever design, Boadicea sets forth all her allurements to win the admiration of Akiba, so that Pappus, his only son and first disciple, puts himself forward as a scapegoat to save his father from danger.

The interference of Pappus is kinder than successful. It does not succeed, and Boadicea, checked in no way by Rufus, becomes so charmed by the attempt to win Akiba to herself, that she willingly consents to be given over to him altogether.

Akiba hears the proposition; spits on the floor, laughs, and weeps. Spits, because the woman, like a drop of impure water, deserves to be expelled from him; laughs, because she wishes to be transformed into a Jewess; weeps, because a person so attractive must fade; for, in spite of himself, he is strangely affected by her devotion to him, and by her beauty.

So Boadicea remains by the side of Rufus, the Tyrian damsel has to go back to Tyre, and Akiba holds the mastery of the field, having won from Rufus permission to open one of his schools in the Holy City of Jerusalem, a second at Bither, a few miles south of Jerusalem, and a third at another Bither which lies on the north of the Sea of Galilee, not far from the Great Sea, and within easy reach of Phœnicia.

CHAPTER XI.

AN AMBASSADOR FROM CÆSAR.

THE permission granted Akiba to open a school in the three centres named in the last chapter carries that wonderful scholar to the Holy City in order to superintend the work he has in hand.

The selection of the sites of these new schools is admirably chosen for strategical purposes. Jerusalem is an historical centre of the utmost value. Bither, to the south of Jerusalem, sometimes called Bither the 'house of spies,' is a place where Jewish sentinels can note and report, along the line of a great highway to the Holy City, who are and who are not favourable to the Roman rule. The other Bither, to the north, north of the Sea of Galilee, Bither, 'the house of liberty,' is a place little known in history, and little thought of by the Roman authorities.

The Sanhedrin continues to sit at Joppa, but Jerusalem now becomes the centre of activity amongst the young Jews who have passed through the hands of their master.

To test the loyalty of Jerusalem, Hadrian, probably at the suggestion of Fortunatus, sends to it a colony of Greeks and Romans, and with the colony a statue of Jupiter to be erected on the site of the once famous Jewish temple. It is a hazardous experiment, and creates the extremest anger amongst all the Jewish community, of whatever sect it may be composed. So angry and fierce are the passions raised that Rufus is in hourly fear of rebellion; and Akiba, who is most anxious not yet to proceed to any extremity, is obliged to labour, by night and by day, in order to quell what would be a serious but abortive effort ending in the most awful effusion of blood and infliction of torture on the Jewish people.

In the difficulty another bright idea occurs to Rufus. He and Akiba are friends, but Akiba must not carry his friendship for him too far, lest it appear that the two are in collusion. The idea is that he, Rufus, should have a new adviser, and he recalls as the person most eligible the powerful and popular Antinous.

Antinous is ever a friend of the Jewish people; Antinous is full of resource, and will be sure to see a way by which all the contentions between Roman and Jew can be reconciled.

A petition is therefore forwarded to the Emperor, praying him to come personally if possible, but if that be impossible, to let the faithful Antinous be despatched as his ambassador.

The reply to this petition is brought from Rome, by Cæsarea, to Jerusalem by Antinous in person. The Emperor wills that the ambassador shall be received with the honour due to Cæsar, and for once Romans and Jews join in what is a public festival. An escort of Roman soldiers, accompanied by Rufus, meets Antinous two leagues from the Holy City, and with great ceremony leads the ambassador onwards to the headquarters of the embassy, situated on a neutral spot apart alike from the Roman garrison and the Jewish quarters. As Jerusalem is approached the enthusiasm is intensified; arches made of palm-boughs are erected, and women with cymbals and men with trumpets and stringed instruments of music welcome the representative of Cæsar.

The Roman for the moment forgets that he is a Roman, the Jew that he is a Jew.

Before the pavilion which is erected for the temporary home of the ambassador, the Governor of Palestine with his suite, and the chief of the Sanhedrin with the selected of his colleagues and scholars, meet on terms of equality and friendship. They do not, it is true, sit together or eat together, but the two leading authorities exchange complimentary visits and discuss what shall be the order of proceedings when the eagerly expected ambassador appears before them.

The arrival is a scene of great excitement. As the cortège enters, Rufus with Boadicea and Servien, who, with Lucilla, has come from Joppa to take part in the proceedings, advance to Antinous and pay their homage. Akiba and his court follow, and bending very low, so that the fore part of their long gaberdines trails on the ground, offer a welcome as hearty as it is profound. They pray in the Latin tongue, audibly, that the God of their Fathers may be with their illustrious visitor in all goings out and comings in.

Antinous bows acknowledgment; before dismounting rides between the two groups who have given such warm welcome to the elect of Cæsar; and then in a clear, resonant, and unfaltering voice speaks.

THE SPEECH OF ANTINOUS.

'Friends of Jerusalem, Jews and Romans alike, friends I trust of my august master Cæsar, my mission is to bring to you peace. The last words from Cæsar's lips to me were: " Peace, happiness, amity amongst all my people in the ancient city of the Jews and in all the borders of Palestine."

'Jews! Romans! Greeks! friends all of whatsoever rank or sect you are, I greet you in the name of Cæsar. To the Jews I am the bearer from my master of a special message. Some months since, in order to try your loyalty to Rome, he sent a statue of the great god of the Romans, to be erected on the site of your most sacred place. He bids me now, as the first act of his confidence and grace, remove that statue and send it to a Roman temple.'

The loud cries of '*Ave Cæsar!*' from the Jewish voices spent, Antinous continues:—

'But, O Jews, in this act of grace remember, I pray you, the confidence and beneficence of Hadrian, and let his practice be your example. The ancient gods of Rome are as dear to him as your God is to you. Be you therefore tolerant to those who differ from you about the gods as he is tolerant to you. It is his will that all men in Jerusalem, in Palestine, in every part where Rome rules, shall be free to worship as they may wish, to live as they may desire, to enjoy trade and commerce, to follow their own customs and usages, and in all things, subject to the laws of Rome, which Romans obey, be free and happy.

'Ave Cæsar!'

If the latter part of this address be less applauded by the Jews than the first it meets with no obvious disfavour from them, while by Greeks, Romans, Egyptians, and others outside the Jewish pale it is accepted with loudest acclamations.

The speech delivered, Rufus and Akiba attend upon the handsome ambassador. Akiba gives the ambassador his hand with serene and elevated dignity amounting to admiration as he sees the youthfulness of the face and the pure features of one of his own people. His bright eyes pierce those of the stranger, and the unseen pressure of the hand of the stranger sends the blood through his heart until he is well-nigh confused. There is help for Israel in that pressure which he has never felt before.

In the choicest Hebrew he responds to the pressure with the words:

> 'Pray for the peace of Jerusalem:
> They shall prosper that love thee.'

And his heart still more strongly throbs as his ear catches the response in the same tongue:

> 'For my brethren and companions' sake I will say,
> Peace be within thee.
> Because of the house of the Lord our God
> I will seek thy good.'

Then to a Greek, who presents a golden chaplet, the ambassador offers, in the Ionic dialect, grateful thanks for so graceful a gift.

Finally, Rufus, who is holding the stirrup, and Servien, who is placing the carpet on which the rider is to alight, are greeted with most cordial recognition, spoken in bold and manly Latin, followed by the usual kiss of friendship, which so pleases Rufus that, having taken it on one of his fat and ruddy cheeks, he offers the other also, as if he particularly enjoyed this particular part of the ceremony. Boadicea is jealous. She has never before known Rufus kissed twice at the same interview by any person. One of the kisses certainly belonged to her.

It is a day of great rejoicing in the city of Jerusalem. Jupiter has been removed from the site of the holy place and set up in the Roman temple, where he seems to be far more at home. The priests of the temple declare that, on being enshrined over their altar, the stern features of the god relaxed and assumed a beneficent aspect. It is certain that the features are modified when the people are readmitted to sacrifice after all the alterations connected with the enshrinement are complete. The Jupiter, so severe on the site of the old Jewish temple, has become a benign Jupiter in his new place and amongst his own worshippers. His hard, short, straight, dumb lips have assumed a gentle downward curve amounting almost to a smile.

Jupiter is content, and is the pride of his priests; the miracle which has transformed him is a constant theme of gratification to them, in which Rufus joins with all his jovial heart.

Some are good enough to say that the aspect of Jupiter is somewhat toned to that of Rufus himself; but these, perhaps, are sycophants.

Boadicea is sure they are, though they may even be priests of Jupiter. Rufus is not so sure, for he knows the jealous nature of his critic. Had the statue been that of Juno, and had it become changed into a likeness of Boadicea, there would, he says, 'have been no sycophants then.' This is told to Servien, who, having observed, in his honest blundering way, that 'no change would have been necessary, seeing how naturally Boadicea is like to the statue of Juno,' gets for reply that his entrance on the service of that goddess would be a good exchange of service for Rome; a rude joke, which he would fain repel if he dared offend the Governor of Palestine.

Is the great assembly which so warmly greets Antinous universally deceived?

Does no one recognise, behind the knight of Rome and favourite of Hadrian, Huldah the child of Cæsarea, the divine maiden of the camp of Silurian Britain?

On this point Rufus is somewhat haunted with a kind of mysterious and ghostly admonition, the nature of which he does not fully understand. He imagines over and over again that there is something peculiar, but what it is is the puzzle. If he were industrious enough he might work it out, but he is not industrious, and therefore takes refuge in the excuse to himself that, whatever it is, as it is not his business it had better be left without interference or trouble on his part.

Akiba is not wanting in industry, and is also strangely impressed, but for the moment is led away by a side thought. He feels quite sure that he has seen the face before, but connects the memory with one of his early pupils whom he has not met for many years. More than once the suspicion crosses him that it is the long-lost Simeon, the Son of a Star himself, and do what he may he cannot help connecting the noble stranger with his divine protégé. But as he studies the face the idea recedes from him. One shadow of a guess as to the true sex of the ambassador and all would be clear to him as the sun at noon, but the well-practised impersonation of Antinous is much too good to give him this chance of enlightening his mental darkness.

For all the rest, as they have no reason for being deceived, they doubt not for a moment that Antinous is Antinous.

All, all, except one man, who does not for a moment doubt, who knows as none but he can know the whole truth, who is torn with perfect agony of joy at the discovery he has made, and who is holding communion with his own mind how and when he shall turn his discovery to account.

Amongst those who stood close to Akiba when he gave his hand to the ambassador was this very man, a man of more than middle age, about whom there seemed to be some secret mystery amongst the Jews. He walked with a stoop as if he could not put one foot one foot's space before the other; the sleeves of his gaberdine came down over his hands, and his arms seemed stiflly stretched out; his face was unduly lengthened and marked by signs of an anguish which was absolutely terrible to look upon.

The Romans cast on him the contempt of pity, as a deformity it were well to avoid. The Jews, on the other hand, looked upon him with respect that was kindled into awe; yet no one knew his history.

Obviously he was under the protection of Akiba; some said he was an old servant of Akiba, others that he was a poor relation of that great man. Anyway, he was most rigorously guarded and was sufficiently secure. Once a student of the schools had incited some other students to pull at the gaberdine or robe of this singular being in order to get a look at his hands. The screams of the poor creature roused the whole school, and so alarmed the offenders that they quickly gave up their rude attempt.

Brought before Akiba they were all signally punished, although the insulted man himself pleaded for them. Discipline had been broken and punishment must follow. All the students concerned in the matter were for a time reduced in rank. The ringleader was expelled for two years.

'Akiba,' it is said, 'loves the poor soul. What more need any man want who claims to be a Jew of Jerusalem?'

This man, so soon as Antinous came fairly within his sight, seemed to be transformed. Suddenly, and for the first time in the knowledge of any who knew him, he stood firmly erect.

When the ambassador began to deliver his address the manner of the man underwent a new change; he turned his ear towards the speaker and listened as one listens who is tuning the strings of a harp, moving his head to the cadences of the speaker, and relaxing his expression of countenance until the sad and awful anguish softened into the very radiance of delight. So great was the transformation that some of the Jews thought the man must be in the spirit, and that he would burst forth into prophecy.

When the ambassador closed the address

he had to deliver, the entranced listener, holding his breath, stood motionless, waiting for the next event.

That event was the observation in Hebrew of Antinous to Akiba, and it completed the ecstasy.

As if a new life had been given to the lame man, as if a new body of the noblest form had been given to him, as if a new soul had filled him with the sublimest purpose, he literally reared his broken frame out of the dust and weight that had hitherto oppressed it, and with an exclamation of surprise and adoration to heaven left the group amongst which he was standing and set foot towards the synagogue with the dignity of a high-priest.

Antinous, busied in dismounting and in receiving the introductions of those around, had missed this spectacle, as indeed had most who were there. Intent to cluster near and get a good look at the handsome representative of Cæsar, the majority were too much occupied to note the departure of one person, however much his manner might be changed, while they were standing as an attentive audience absorbed with the one object before them.

Later on, when they met together to discuss the things which they had seen, it was natural enough for some to remark on the curious behaviour of the friend of Akiba, but now it was not in their thoughts.

The man himself is seen no more that day. He remains alone in the house of his Lord, blessing his name and thanking him for all his mercies.

As night steals on he waits still, with perfect satisfaction that some one else will come. He eats not, drinks not, sleeps not, but waits.

The night passes, the morning breaks; the silence is deathly, and still before the altar he stands, inspired by faith as to what must be.

A footstep! a footstep! at the sunrise! A light footstep at the door of the sacred place.

The synagogue is entered and the footstep approaches the altar in the manner he had anticipated. A woman in the vestments of a man is going, by habit, to the women's place in the synagogue. The discovery is all but complete.

One word from him and it is completed.

'Huldah!'

'Elkanah! my Father!'

There are scenes of human passion of unspeakable sorrow, of unspeakable joy, which admit of no description by either pen or pencil, and this scene, during the first stages of it, is of that nature.

'I knew thou wouldst come to Synagogue when the heathen would set thee free,' is the first utterable sentence that can be recorded.

'I knew thou wouldst find the house of the Holy One of Israel.'

'But how canst thou love me, Father, in this disguise?'

'Love thee, Huldah? I worship thee! Keep it, wear it, play thy part in it. It is the Lord's doing, and marvellous in our eyes. Like Joseph in the court of Pharaoh, thou shalt save thy people.'

Hand in hand they sit in the sanctuary and tell their histories, from the moment when they were parted in Cæsarea, where Huldah and the elected Simeon were concealed and Elkanah was dragged forth to be crucified.

'Most strange, my child, most strange! From that moment until I heard thee yesterday I have always been crucified. My limbs have never lost the mortal agony; now they are once more free.

'They left me for dead, my child, they left me for dead, but the death-wine which the Nazarene woman, who was the sister of the Roman centurion, Fidelis, raised to my lips made death a semblance only. In the night the wind blew a hurricane, and with the cross dashed me to the earth. The fall roused me back to life, and out of the cross drove the nail that pierced my right hand. From that hand I wrenched with my teeth the nail, and, one hand free, I soon set myself free altogether. At the foot of the cross I found food and water left by that holy woman. I ate, I was refreshed, but knew not where to go, for Roman soldiers lay in wait in every quarter. Then she appeared, she, that holy Nazarene—Akiba likes me not to call her holy, but I will—and led me to a safe place in a mountain, and fed me there till I could travel to Phœnicia, where, concealing my injuries, I remained as a sorcerer or wise man. Sometimes I wandered in search of thee, but uselessly, for I knew not whether thou wert alive. At length, as the rebellion in Cæsarea became forgotten and I became a thing of the past, I ventured to sail from Tyre to Joppa in a vessel carrying fruit, and so revealed myself to the renowned Akiba, under whose protection I have lived as a reader of our sacred scriptures to the youths of the academy.

'Twas a happy choice of Akiba to give me that duty: it accounted for my bended back; it permitted me to hide my hands in the ample folds of my robe; and it gave me employment that was dearest to my heart.

' Maimed of body, my soul has gone forth in the words I have had to speak, and with them has been borne through every part of our oppressed land. Sometimes I have felt that both the Isaiahs have lived again through me, and that the second, glorious prophet of that name, bearing from me his blessed opening words, " *Comfort ye, comfort ye, my people,*" has echoed them back with his own inspired voice.

' But the sun is rising, my Huldah, my darling, my own. Thou must pray and begone, and I for the allotted time must reassume my misery and my ministry.

'Yet tell me, ere we part, knowest thou aught of Simeon, the coming saviour of Israel?'

In words as brief as they were clear

Elkanah hears the news of Simeon to the latest that is known to Huldah.

It is known where he can be found, which is enough, for the moment, for Elkanah to know.

At the usual hour for reading the sacred scriptures to the new school at Jerusalem Elkanah is at his post. More earnestly than ever he has been heard before, he declaims from his favourite prophet:—

'I have raised up one from the north, and he shall come
From the rising of the sun shall he call upon my name:
And he shall come upon princes as upon mortar,
And as the potter treadeth clay.

The Lord shall go forth as a mighty man,
He shall stir up jealousy like a man of war:
He shall cry, yea, roar;
He shall prevail against his enemies.

I have long holden my peace;
I have been still and refrained myself;
Now will I cry like a travailing woman;
I will destroy and devour at once.

O Zion, that bringest good tidings, get thee up into the
    high mountain;
O Jerusalem, that bringest good tidings,
Lift up thy voice with strength;
Lift it up, be not afraid!
Say unto the cities of Judah,
Behold your God!'

The students are taken as if by storm. The words, by some unseen influence, rise and rise again in their breasts. In their unquenchable zeal they fight the air with their breaths, and are ready to die, with their hearts, for Judah and Jerusalem.

See! see! also in the distance, watching the effect, with courage as high and heart as true as the youngest amongst them, Akiba stands, knowing now much better than they how near is the predicted hour.

And Antinous? Well, Antinous breakfasts with Rufus and Servien, arranges the plans of the day, is charmed by Lucilla, and is very much waited on by Boadicea.

CHAPTER XII.

THE MISSION TO ITS CLOSE.

To Tinnius Rufus and to Servien the mission of Antinous to Palestine is, for the time, successful beyond all expectation. With an effect which is truly astonishing the news of the visit of Antinous passes from city to city, from camp to camp, and from village to village, causing little demonstration or excitement and producing the most tranquillising influence. The rule of Rufus becomes now a rule of peace and comfort, to him altogether unexampled. The change is all his luxurious soul has craved for. He eats the best suppers, drinks the best wines, listens to the best jokes, sleeps the best sleeps, and, in jovial hours, sings songs which so obviously please himself that others are pleased with his pleasure rather than with his performance.

To the Jews Rufus becomes more friendly than Servien likes. Playing from Jerusalem

the part of Herod the Great, he undertakes to
build them a new temple so soon as Cæsar will
give his assent to that grand enterprise. He
promises that Cæsar himself shall visit Palestine with the rest of his Syrian provinces,
and that on his visit the illustrious Akiba shall
lay the foundation-stone of the new temple,
with every kind of ancient ceremonial belonging to the history of the chosen people.

The chosen people listen to these good
tidings with hearts of joy, and they know
their source.

'The words spoken by the lips of Rufus
are from the heart of Antinous.'

Antinous, hearing this expression, corrects
it by requesting to add to it 'and from the
mind of Cæsar.'

Akiba improves the saying by a short
proverb which goes round the land into every
synagogue and into every Jewish home:—
'Cæsar thinks, Antinous feels, Rufus speaks.'

From Jerusalem Antinous proceeds to
Joppa.

In company with Servien, Antinous visits
the Roman forts and earthworks of Joppa, the

ships of war that lie in the harbour, and the roads that lead eastward to Jerusalem, northward to Cæsarea, and southward to the ancient Askelon and Gaza. To each of these points of observation some critical remark is directed. That fort should be strengthened with walls or ditches or moats; this post should have in it a larger or a smaller number of men; there a guardship should lie at anchor; here a harbour should be constructed, to save vessels from being lost on the wild and raking coast. At another point a roadway should be laid out, so as to secure a good landing between the open sea and the solid shore.

Servien does not quite relish the interference between the land and the sea. He knows how useful that unpromising coast-line has been in former times against invading hosts, and how the Jews, in high rebellion against Rome when Cestius was governor, were driven into the sea by their thousands, to perish by the war of the waves and the wrath of the ocean, without the loss of one Roman sword, javelin, or man. But Servien is gently overborne in argument. That which is suggested is from the ambassador of Cæsar, and Lucilla approves, which is an important additional fact. So the order goes forth for all that is suggested to be done forthwith.

Akiba asks that in such benign work his students of the mechanical schools may take part. The permission is granted, and Jew scholar and Roman soldier work for the first time shoulder to shoulder with an earnestness which passes into a friendly contest as to who shall do most. The Jewish scholars bring all kind of theoretical skill to Servien for his practised eye to see and mind to study. They make an abacus, or sand table, at his feet, and one of them draws out with his stylus the changes that he may suggest.

They comply, as it seems to him, with everything he wishes, and they accomplish in the end everything which they themselves have devised and desired. Every touch of artistic work, which adds relief or perfection of form to the forts and walls, they design, but the credit of it, in a natural and unassuming manner, goes to Servien.

Antinous leaves Joppa when the work begins, travels through Northern Palestine to Bither, the 'house of liberty,' makes a complete round of the province, re-enters Jerusalem by Southern Bither, the 'house of spies,' and then, accompanied by Rufus, Boadicea, and Akiba, pays a final visit to Joppa on the way back to Rome.

The Governor of Palestine and his friend the ambassador are equally delighted with the changes which have been made in Joppa by the skill of the youths of the schools, under the direction of Servien. There is Servien's Arch, Servien's Tower, and the fort of Servien; and all Joppa would, indeed, have been Servien's, apparently, if that worthy and modest soldier had not insisted on attaching the names of Hadrian, Rufus, Antinous, and Akiba to his granitic labours. The grand roadway from the sea, the noblest piece of work of all, is therefore named the 'Road of Hadrian,' while the splendid fire tower, that has sprung up as by magic, is the 'Pharos of Rufus,' a name which delights to the last degree the humour of that fiery-headed personage. The harbour would be the harbour of Antinous, but Antinous will have it changed to the harbour of Sabina, after the Empress; the guard-ship at anchor is the Boadicea, 'because of its restless grace,' while the landing-place of all the vessels is Lucilla's Porch, because of its serene and friendly attractions.

Akiba, with trained humility, has declined every honour of the kind; it is opposed to the commandments of his great lawgiver, which forbid that a Jew should make to himself ' any graven image or the likeness of anything that is in the heaven above or in the earth beneath, or in the waters under the earth.'

Before leaving Palestine Antinous returns, with Rufus and his court, to Jerusalem, in order to hold a council. Rufus, Antinous, and Akiba meet and discuss what shall be done in order to maintain the good understanding which now prevails between the rulers and the ruled in every part of Palestine.

The consultation leads to an edict which, subject to the approval of Hadrian, shall hold good towards all the people under the governance of Rufus, by the supreme will of the Emperor. The edict is extremely voluminous, for Rufus will insist on giving it the character of a State document of such historical importance that it shall survive his beneficent rule and make him the admired of Jews as well as Romans for all time.

To please the Jews, moreover, without directly conveying the intention to them, he has the edict drawn out in ten distinct parts or sections, like a new decalogue, a design which in some Judaical tempers might have cost him his life as a blasphemy, but which at the present moment is accepted with a good nature amounting to nothing worse than a mock serenity, because, says Akiba, 'ten is a wise and useful number.

'Man works with ten fingers and walks on ten toes.

'He has ten conspicuous parts of his body: two eyes, two ears, two lips, two hands, two feet.

'He performs ten great functions: he eats, drinks, breathes, walks, talks, plays, works, sleeps, wakes, and prays.

'He has ten great blessings: sun, moon, stars, air, water, food, raiment, fire, house, and land.

'He has ten choice friends: father, mother, teacher, brother, sister, wife, son, daughter, servant, and neighbour.

'He has ten noble virtues: love, truth, courage, industry, justice, faith, generosity, honour, knowledge, and wisdom.

'He has the ten Holy Commandments.

'These are the seven great tens, the last the greatest; and whosoever holds them all is blessed. Therefore is ten a wise and useful number, and if the edict be sound, it is well and thoughtfully divided.'

The edict, thus divided, ran as follows:—

AN EDICT SUGGESTED TO CÆSAR BY TINNIUS RUFUS, GOVERNOR OF PALESTINE.

I.

That all peoples, races, and tongues in Palestine, subject always to the common laws of the Empire, shall have perfect and equal freedom with Roman citizens.

II.

That all sects of religion shall enjoy equal rights to worship in their own fashion and according to their own ceremonies, provided that no man shall interfere with another, nor attempt to draw others into his own pale.

III.

That Jews resident in Palestine shall, on payment of a tax to be named by Cæsar, be exempt from the necessity of offering divine sacrifice to Cæsar by the burning of incense or other form of worship.

IV.

That the site of the Holy Temple at Jerusalem shall be enclosed, and shall be left as a place sacred to the Jewish people waiting its restoration for the services of their faith.

V.

That the Grand Sanhedrin, now holding its seat at Joppa, shall be permitted to return to Jerusalem whenever it shall desire to effect that change.

VI.

That the Jews shall have equal rights with the Romans to petition the Emperor on all questions in which they feel they are unjustly treated.

VII.

That in matters coming strictly under Jewish ordinance, every Jew who voluntarily lives in obedience to such ordinance shall be tried by his own people on every charge that does not imply sedition or treason against Rome as the acknowledged ruling authority.

VIII.

That Jews belonging to other sects, Nazarenes, Ebionites, Essenes, Gnostics, shall in like manner be governed by the laws of their own orders, if they prefer to be judged by them rather than by the Roman courts.

IX.

That the tribute to Cæsar shall be levied equally on all his loyal subjects, whatever may be their race— Romans, Jews, Greeks, Syrians, Egyptians, or others.

x.

That under the direction of the Grand Sanhedrin schools for the Jewish youths may be established in any part of Palestine, as at Joppa, subject to the order that no weapons of war, no military exercises, and nothing of any kind that shall lead to armed revolt, be practised in the schools.

The promulgation of the news that these proposals are about to be submitted to the Emperor by his chosen ambassador, and with the assent of the Roman governor and of Servien, is a cause of universal satisfaction in the whole of the subdued province.

Rufus becomes the most popular of governors, and Antinous is greeted as a deliverer of the people.

The time has now arrived when Antinous must return to Rome; and in Jerusalem, the first scene of departure, there is universal sorrow. Whatever may have been the former differences between the Romans and the Jews, these are forgotten; the regret that the beloved Antinous must go away can never be forgotten.

Out of Jerusalem the ruddy Rufus rides in his chariot with a splendid escort of horsemen, and with the ambassador by his side, for three furlongs on the road to Joppa. They are followed by an immense multitude, and when they part a multitude still continues to follow, some even to Joppa itself.

Out of Joppa the people march with Servien at their head, to meet the ambassador with Akiba and the rest coming from Jerusalem. To the surprise of all, Elkanah, the reader of the synagogue, is seen in bright attire, mounted on a camel; he is as one possessed of a new life, as one inspired, now weeping, now rejoicing, and then offering up prayers and supplications for mercies to come.

'See,' they say, 'even the reader of Akiba, who was never known to show any emotion, weeps at the departure of Antinous more than the rest, and in this new affliction forgets his affliction of old.'

For three days Antinous rests in the house of Servien, and quits it with a grief that cannot be concealed. But the galley lies waiting, the winds are propitious, and the ambassador must indeed depart back to Cæsar. Servien, Lucilla, Akiba and all the notabilities, with crowds of scholars and people, go to the place of embarkation.

A long time is taken up in farewells, and two notable events are specially observed.

Eli, the trusted and beloved attendant and companion of the ambassador, Eli, called by common consent the second Anak, is left behind in the care of Akiba, and the last person who receives the fervent farewell and closest embrace is the once-deformed reader, who no longer walks foot by foot, with arms outstretched and back bent, but who stands forth with a noble carriage and all but rivals Akiba in dignity as, with saddened faces, the two follow, side by side, to the margin of the sea. A blast of trumpets gives the signal that Antinous is planted on the sea; another blast tells that the imperial galley with the golden prow is safely reached.

The sails of the galley are set to the wind, the standard of Rome is let loose and floats proudly; the galley slaves bring the oars in line; a shout from the shore; a return shout from the galley; a dash of every oar, as if it were a single oar, into the waves; a steady pull far, far into the distance, and the parting is over.

Antinous stands alone in the stern of the vessel, whilst Akiba and the transformed Elkanah stand like statues on the shore in the foreground of the host that watches the galley melt away until it and its precious freight remain a mere memory of the past.

CHAPTER XIII.

ANTINOUS NO MORE.

The ambassador to Palestine has performed the embarrassing mission directed by the Emperor in a manner as faithfully as successfully. To play the part of the knight Antinous and of Huldah the daughter of Elkanah has been an effort which few who ever lived could have played, and which none who ever lived could have played with more consummate judgment, skill, and loyalty. As a political task it is known to the master of all the legions of Rome and approved of by him. It has therefore in it, in so far as the chief actor is concerned, no sin and no shame. Whatever may happen, the responsibility must be accepted by Cæsar.

Antinous—for as yet it is best to use the assumed name—has all through been moved by two contending forces: one of loyalty to the chosen people, the other of loyalty to Cæsar.

As a matter of natural necessity, these two parts could not fairly be balanced ; as a matter of natural necessity, home and kindred and country held the first place, for they were first implanted in the heart and had deepest root there. But Cæsar, as Hadrian, could not at the same time be forgotten or ill-treated. Cæsar, who has so graciously made Antinous Antinous, must be obeyed and honoured.

By pressure between these contending influences the mind of the ambassador is brought to a new and critical position.

Palestine and Hadrian may and must be equally loved and saved ; Rome, as a force apart from the Emperor, may be hated, and in due time and season opposed and conquered.

Suppose the Emperor Hadrian were deposed, abdicated, or dead ; what, then, is Rome to a daughter of Israel ?

Akiba and Elkanah both know this position, and both support it. It is a part of that subtlety which passes in their minds for wisdom.

For the present the proposed edict of

Rufus meets many difficulties, unless something quite unforeseen should suddenly transpire. If it be carried out in full it is all so much in favour of the Jews in Palestine that it may quiet their patriotic longings for many a long day, and leave them ready to proclaim their own independence should the power of Rome begin to wane. The acts of Hadrian have shown already that, in his opinion, the conquering hand of Rome has been carried too far by the fighting Trajan. Perhaps Rome has gone on to victory further than is safe, and, ruined by wars with distant foes and drained of men, may one day soon be glad to come to terms with a friendly people and grant an autonomy to the Jews of the Holy Land.

The hope is reasonable, and is also reasonably honest; but, with the exception of that part which permits the extension of the schools, and which, on the ground of precedent, Rufus himself takes the responsibility of permitting, nothing is done. The Jews must wait for Cæsar.

When Antinous returns to Rome, Hadrian, the soul of the Empire, is in the throes of one of the severest fits of despondency from which he has ever suffered. His mind is oppressed with the idea of the utter valuelessness of life and the absolute vanity of the highest, the most exalted, the most successful human ambition. He demands the right to die. He calls upon Tryphon to give him 'morion,' death-wine, that he, like the many wretched creatures on the cross, may depart in peace from a world which is to him a prolonged and agonising crucifixion. He cannot rest, he cannot sleep, he cannot work. His judgment is as clear as ever; his reasoning powers are not diseased, but his animal life is virtually dead, and his emotional life is a sea of trouble. He is afflicted with panic about nothing at all; some impending evil or sorrow, the nature of which he cannot define, is ever upon him; the blackness of death grows white to his ideal eyes whenever the blackness of life comes under his contemplation.

Tryphon, fairly unable to cope with such despairing gloom, prays for no one so much as Antinous, and Hadrian on his part counts the seconds for the arrival of his ambassador. Courier after courier is despatched to hasten

Antinous home, and all the Court waits in expectation.

'One word from Antinous will be worth more than Esculapius himself,' says the Empress Sabina, as with the young and growing favourite Marcus Antoninus she discusses the Emperor's last words in the delirium from which he suffers.

At last the healing and long-expected messenger arrives, and hastens to the side of the Ruler of the legions, the Prince of the whole world.

What is the magic which some of the human race possess? Why does the same word which from one mouth is meaningless or despicable become a word of healing and confidence from another mouth that may be much less learned and even less honest and truthful?

It is impossible to answer.

Antinous faces the despairing Cæsar, taking him by surprise at a moment when he is depressed almost to the death for which he is imploring.

'How well my gracious lord looks!' This is the first greeting.

'*Well*, my Antinous! I am sick to desperation, killed with black care, darker, denser than the most wretched horseman ever carried at his back. *Atra cura*—black care—*Atra cura*, my Antinous, bears me to the earth.'

'*Atra cura* is not the word for Cæsar, whose face bears a light of health and youth which I have never seen before. *Atra cura* belongs rather to thy Antinous, who, alarmed by the message he has received, has rested neither day nor night until the wearied eyes should witness that men had been deceived and that Cæsar was never more ready for new work and new enterprise than now.'

It is enough. Under the impression that his favourite is suffering for his sake, Hadrian instantly forgets his own anxieties. He who a moment ago was the patient becomes the physician.

Tryphon, unable to repress the smile he throws at his clever ally, falls into the humour. Antinous must have every care. Cæsar is convalescent; it is Antinous that must be looked after. Food, wine, rest, pastime—all for Antinous.

The Emperor and Tryphon are in daily consultation, in which the Empress joins.

The Emperor asks what more can be done that Antinous may recover.

'Hast thou, great Tryphon, no restorative in all thy treasury of medicaments that can save such a life?'

'Antinous, Prince, has told me the sovereign remedy. It is the medicine for the mind that he requires. If Cæsar would condescend to lead Antinous to some new scene all would soon be well.'

'And where is the scene that would suit the best?'

'Egypt, the land of wonders. The land of the mighty Pharaohs, the land which Moses, Alexander, Herodotus, Cyrus, Plato, Pliny, studied with such devoted ardour, and in which Hadrian might also find the choicest treasures of his Empire.'

'So let it be. It has long been the desire of Hadrian's heart to visit Egypt with Antinous.

'Let no time be lost, we will go to the land of marvels. Let every scholar, every architect, every philosopher, every sculptor, every artist, every writer, every artisan who belongs to the travelling cortège of Cæsar, prepare for Egypt.'

'The cheek of Antinous revives under the thought of the journey,' is the report of Tryphon each morning to his Imperial master.

And the cheek of the master revives also.

'The healing gifts of Antinous have returned,' is another report of the subtle Tryphon to the delighted Cæsar.

'When are we ready for the journey?'

'All are ready.'

Nothing, so far, could be more propitious. Hadrian, forgetting all his own sorrows, dedicates to his friend the poem soon to be well known as '*Cor non edito*' ('Eat not thine heart.')

COR NON EDITO.

Eat not thine heart, with care:
  The gods are kind
To all who bravely bear
  The equal mind,
And cast their cares behind.

Eat not thine heart, with dread:
  The gods supply
Each man with living bread
  Who dares rely
Upon his destiny.

Eat not thine heart, with grief:
　The gods will bring
To the pure soul relief
　From evil thing
　That unto it may cling.

Eat not thine heart, with thought:
　The gods ordain
No mind shall e'er be bought
　Or sold, for gain,
　That would to theirs attain.

Marching to Neapolis the travellers set sail for Alexandria, and for some weeks stay there, in the home of light and knowledge.

Alexandria is divided, physically and mentally, into classes or sections. The Jews have their part of the city, the Romans and Greeks theirs, the Egyptians theirs. These form what may be considered three distinct schools of thought, a social triangle the base of which is Egyptian, one side Græco-Roman and the other Hebraic.

The sections live in learned amity: the disputes they hold are often keen, but they do not disturb the general good feeling which has long prevailed in the memories of the great men who have lived in the city of learning. Greeks, Romans, and Egyptians alike refer with pride to the learned Philon Judæus, whose work, 'The Heir of Divine Things,' is still popular; Jews and Egyptians agree in respecting the memory of Pompey notwithstanding his onslaught on Jerusalem, while they equally lament the unfortunate siege of Cæsar, which led to the accidental destruction by fire of that great library of the Museum which held a copy of every known book in all the known world. And Greeks, Romans, and Jews alike agree in their admiration of the wisdom and learning and industry of ancient Egypt, the mother of their souls.

Still in one of the courts of the magnificent temple of Serapis is a library of half a million volumes saved from the assault of Cæsar; not, alas, the choicest of the book treasures in the once famous Museum, but still a world in itself of the inspiration of mankind.

Hadrian is now in a sphere which is to him the richest and the best. He is at home. He forgets his own ailments; he rejoices to see that Antinous is happy; he resides in a part of the temple of Serapis itself, that he may be near the renowned library, and there, irrespective of creed or race, he discusses things past, present, and to come with all the learned and the wise.

Access is denied to no scholar. The student of the Eleusinian mysteries is here at home with the Emperor, and teaches even the Emperor much in which he delights. The Egyptian priest recounts to him the mystery of Horus, the child god, representing Osiris, who descended from heaven, who became incarnate; who opposed the dark spirit of evil; who, after working astounding miracles, laid down his life for man, was buried, rose again, and ascending back to his immortal mansions, by his immortal part, left his body in the tomb of the holy island, the tomb of the 'opener of good,' and the 'judge of the living and the dead.'

In like manner the Cæsar listens to the Gnostic mystic who combines the Egyptian ritual and faith with the Jewish traditions; who clothes the Eternal power in light and glory, and in noble poetry carries the soul of man himself out of its mortal garb of flesh, even at the will of man, into the pleuroma or region of celestial and immortal life. Nor is so simple and genuine a man as the pure Galilean or Nazarene forbidden the presence of the Emperor. No; he, too, finds Cæsar ready not merely to listen to his record or gospel, but, struck by its simplicity and beauty, to propose to the silent horror of the gospeller, that the grand central figure of that gospeller's narrative should be placed like one of the gods of Rome in a shrine or temple erected to his honour in the holy Jerusalem.

To the Jews of the old and orthodox faith of their fathers he shows, moreover, a condescension which no previous Cæsar has ever shown before. Antinous and Tryphon are at hand to suggest what is good for their people, and by casual and yet judicious words pour into his bosom the patriotic sentiments which are implanted most deeply in their own natures.

The Emperor goes even to the grand synagogue : witnesses the classes of the guilds and the council of the Elders ; listens to the soul-stirring service, and, lost in the enthusiasm which follows the singing of the glorious psalm :—

'The heavens declare the glory of the Lord,'

lends his own voice to the loud Alleluiah, and directs that the poem shall be written out for him in letters of gold, that he may himself translate it into Roman verse.

That this enthusiasm of Hadrian is merely a sign of his emotional nature ; that it does not reside in his retentive and reasoning soul, is clear enough from the observation he afterwards made, and which has been already recorded.

While, however, the enthusiasm is upon him, the opportunity is excellent for placing before him the proposed edict of Rufus. Antinous has prepared the way by recounting to him at opportune moments the events of the late journey through Palestine, and when the document is duly placed before him he gives to it his most careful perusal. Not only so, but he very cordially approves of it as a whole, and expresses the pleasure it will give him to visit Palestine personally and to have a medal struck in honour of the visit, in which he shall be depicted holding out the olive branch of peace to a symbolised Conqueror of Judea, bearing a likeness to the countenance of the handsome ambassador who has served the cause of Israel so well and so wisely.

An artist accompanying the Emperor is duly instructed to prepare the design of the medal, and executes the order so promptly and so much to the pleasure of Cæsar, that the medal is struck in anticipation of the impending tour.

The projected design so far exceeds all expectation; but—there is often a 'but' in matters of greatest moment—one difficulty intervenes: a postponement from a cause that is inevitable.

Hadrian from the very commencement of his reign has shown an almost superstitious deference to the wishes and decisions of the Senate. For that august body itself he does not really and intrinsically care 'a worn-out sandal;' a fact he would show to it in an hour if it presumed to question his absolute authority. But—there is that wonderful 'but' again—it answers his sovereign pleasure to assume a respect which, although but childish, serves his purpose. In his absence the Senate governs through the Empress, and as it is his wish to be absent from Rome whenever he likes and as long as he likes, it is excellent policy to trust the Senate.

The Senate in return trusts him. Let an upstart claimant to the throne appear while he is away, and there is the Senate sitting for Hadrian.

The Senate is Cæsar and Cæsar is the Senate.

In personal consultation with the Senate the will of Cæsar is the will of the Senate. Away from Rome the will of the Senate is the will of Cæsar.

On this important matter, therefore, the Senate must be consulted. The whole business is a farce, that Antinous and Tryphon know perfectly, but it must be complied with. No law of Mede or Persian is more unalterable than that law.

So the edict must wait. It is not much of a compromise after all. The journey through Egypt will soon be over; the sojourn afterwards in Rome need not be for long; and then will come the triumphant march through the Holy Land and, it may be, the reconstruction of the Holy Temple for the children of the Lord in the land of promise flowing with milk and honey.

The Imperial travellers pursue their way

through the mysteries of Egypt. Proceeding along the Nile they arrive at Heliopolis, where they rest to see the wonderful seat of learning at which so many of the great lights of the ancient world have lived and studied. Heliopolis is no longer the school of schools, but much remains to be observed which gives to the place an undying glory. Here still stands the house of Plato, or the house where he resided when, in the prime of his life, he travelled to the first academy of the earth and took his lessons there. Athens has long since been more famous than Heliopolis, and Rome is rising into rivalry with Athens, but both these came from this sacred spot. What Rome is to Athens, Athens once was to Heliopolis.

And if there were nothing more in Heliopolis than one simple thing, that simple thing is worth all the journey—the obelisk of Osirtasen.

The obelisk, constructed of granite, is over two thousand years of age. On two sides of it is an inscription written fully twenty centuries ago, and perfect now as ever. The pride of Hadrian is touched. Shall he,

Emperor of the world, remain a pillar of history for as many centuries as this dead monolith? What ages yet may it not last? What great king placed it where it stands and ordered it to be inscribed upon?

Let this visit to the granite column be recorded and take its chance of history.

From Heliopolis, the city of the sun, the travellers wander to the great Pyramids and the immortal Sphinx, then along the river to the mighty Thebes, the centre of the temples of the living and the dead.

In the region of Thebes Hadrian lives another new life. He is one of the greatest monarchs who has ever reigned. His kingdom, in the minds of his people, is the whole earth, and he himself, notwithstanding his travels by land and sea, has seen it most imperfectly. The place which he now visits is his dominion. If anybody at any time can stand by or in the temple palaces and say these are mine, Hadrian is that man. He can by his mere will command that any one of them shall be his living residence; he can by decree equally command that any one of the temples of the dead shall be his tomb.

In the days of the Pharaohs one-third of the land of Egypt belonged to the reigning Pharaoh, one-third to the priests of the temples, one-third to the soldiers who maintained the dominion of the king. At this moment Hadrian can still claim the rents or dues of one-third of the lands held by the people in bondage under him, as in the ancient time. A fifth of the value of all produce is his, as it was of Rameses the Great.

Hadrian is more than Rameses; he is the Imperator, the leader of the army of Rome, the absolute holder and distributor of that living engine of power. Hadrian is, therefore, the virtual owner of another third of Egypt, and if the priests be disloyal he can easily grasp their third and take the whole.

Cæsar is Egypt and Egypt is Cæsar.

But the august presence of the past in these dwellings of the still living dead is more than Hadrian can bear. He requires no standard-bearer here to whisper in his ear, 'Remember, thou art but a man.' He feels the fact from head to foot, his eyes transmit it to his brain, and he trembles under the impression.

What art thou, Hadrian the Spaniard,

raised by the intrigues of a woman and the voices of a few soldiers into a throne made for thee? What art thou by the side of Rameses the Great and Memnon and Sethos and the rest of the mighty monarchs who built these palaces of life and death?

Thou art a fool, Hadrian, a mere adventurer, a corsair on the sea of time. Hide thyself, man, from the light of history beneath the foot of Rameses the Great.

A visit to the eastern colossus of Thebes, the vocal Memnon of the third Amunoph, completes the impressions thus made upon his mind. He is fain to be away; he is seized with the idea that some of the incomprehensible masses of pillars and arches of the temples will fall upon him and crush him into dust, and this sense of impending physical risk begins to haunt him in his sleep. Yet must he see the colossus of Memnon, and, if possible, hear the voice that speaks from its stony heart.

The priests of the vocal figure of stone are ready for Cæsar.

With becoming awe they prostrate themselves before him. What is their poor statue, dead and cold, to living, burning Cæsar? What is the hollow voice that rings out a sound for a few cubits' length from the statue to the voice that rings over the whole earth?

Come, mighty Cæsar, come and listen to the voice of Memnon! Let the Cæsar that was, the Cæsar of three thousand years agone, exchange speech with the living Cæsar of to-day.

Could Tryphon and Antinous have their own way, the twelfth Cæsar of Rome would not listen to the voice of Amunoph the Third of Egypt. They know too well the effect the voice will have on the impressionable mind of him they serve, and whose love of the marvellous is the weakest greatness of all his greatnesses. Moreover, they are both clever enough and subtle enough to entertain a huge suspicion that the voice is a cheat, a juggle as deep as all that adoration and prostration which the priests of Memnon are now acting so intently to Cæsar.

On this matter, however, they are powerless. If the love of the marvellous inherent in their master were broken, their own power were also broken. After all, they are what the priests are. Shall diamond cut diamond?

A grand array of priests stands around the eastern colossus of Thebes, the vocal Memnon, to receive the Cæsar.

They have erected an altar of stone at the base of the figure. Upon the altar they offer their incense to the 'Ruler of the earth.' They chant a hymn to Memnon and to Cæsar:

The Hymn to Memnon.

God of Egypt! god of Ages!
    Wake to life thy heart of stone;
Whilst another god engages
    To thy voice to lend his own.

Let thy priests, who humbly fear thee,
    Pray thee speak, if but a word;
Lest the god who comes to hear thee
    Draw out his avenging sword.

Hark! the god of night attending
    To the prayers his servants pray;
Now a gracious ear is lending
    To his brother, god of day!

The words, explained to Hadrian by Tryphon, who knows the language in which they are sung, are as grateful to the vanity of the

Imperial genius as they are singular to his sense, for under some circumstances Hadrian is as vain as under other circumstances he seems careless of praise or diffident in respect to it. In plain truth he is always vain, but as he soon tires of everything that is often repeated, he wearies of honours and of adulation that come upon him in repetition.

It is a novelty of adulation to be coupled in name and qualities with Memnon, and therefore it is for the moment a delight to his mind.

The priests follow up their chant by a kind of prayer said in reverent posture with the head bent, the arms crossed over the breast, and the face directed to the east. They then separate into two columns, through which the Emperor is led by the chief of them to the base of the statue.

'Who art thou,' asks Cæsar, 'that has spoken through the ages?'

In an instant there rings out from the seemingly dead statue the sound of a silver and musical tongue, so clear that none could mistake it. To the Emperor it replies, distinctly and resonantly, in answer to his question :—

'Memnon.'

'Dost thou know my name?'

In a sharper but more prolonged strain there comes again an answer which he translates unmistakably.

'Kæsar.'

'To what place am I bound to go from hence?'

Once more an answer, round, ringing, positive, though perhaps rather abbreviated, as if the final vowel were deficient or softened:

'Roma.'

Henceforth the statue is dumb. It has never before been known to answer the same voice three times.

The Emperor is escorted back to his courtiers; the priests surround the statue and recommence their prayers. Again, in honour of their guest, they cast incense on the temporary altar.

The scene is over, and Hadrian is content.

In the marvellous court of Osiris, of the temple palace of Rameses the Great, the Emperor fixes his Imperial quarters. This palace, which contained the library of ancient Egypt ages before the libraries of Alexandria were known—the library called literally 'the medicine of the mind'—is now the veritable possession of the master of the world. Rameses himself was not more the ruler here than Hadrian, and yet Hadrian is not at home. The statue of Rameses is still the master. Its present owner knows and feels himself to be a stranger; a curiosity seeker; a possessor who has no business in his own regal possessions.

Not until he finds himself in his poor soldier's tent, pitched in the grand court of Osiris, and shut off from that sublime and mysterious temple, is Hadrian at home and at peace.

Even then, when darkness falls, the spirits of the awful past haunt him so fiercely that the faithful Tryphon must sleep within speaking distance and use all his consummate skill of speech to while away the time and break the sleepless spell.

'Let the scholars try to translate the writings on these palace walls,' is the order of Cæsar, suggested by Antinous.

Tryphon leads the way to the task, and Hadrian follows with seven scholars more, including Antinous, like the nine scholars of Rameses.

There must be a key to the whole literature of these walls.

Who shall find the key?

It is a test of learning that creates the keenest interest and the highest intellectual activity.

The key is found : the sagacity of Antinous discovers it. All anxieties, all fears of the past fade away. The learned army of Hadrian has conquered a kingdom, a world, the like of which has never been conquered before.

The era of Hadrian shall rival that of the first Cæsar, of Augustus, of Vespasian. It shall open a lost treasury. Alexander shall be nowhere as a conqueror by the side of Hadrian. The secrets of the pyramids, of the temples, of the sphinx, of the vocal Memnon shall all be his own.

Whether any marked progress would have been made in the interpretation of the Egyptian mysteries is unknown. The fates decree that the labour shall cease before it has fairly commenced, and when the fates decree even Hadrians obey.

Again a message from Rome by special bearer to Cæsar.

The Senate prays, 'Return! return! return!'

The danger is imminent. Once more the Jews of Cyprus are the trouble. Under the hand of a fierce Roman oppressor they have been massacred in one of their synagogues. They have risen in response, have fought like lions at bay, preferring rather to die than to live. They have gained what amounts to a practical victory, and on their parts have retaliated with fearful vengeance on Roman men, women, and children.

The news of their sufferings and of their temporary triumph has reached Judea, waiting anxiously for the Emperor's sanction to the edict, and irritated by the delay. Rufus has lost his presence of mind, and is relying on the army rather than on diplomacy. There is a rumour that the advent of the long-expected Star of Jacob, the deliverer, the Messiah of the Jews, has been proclaimed; that the loyalty of the great Akiba is doubted; and that Servien is resolute on repression, but irresolute when and where to begin that gloomy and doubtful process.

'May it please the Emperor at once to return and guide the counsels of Rome by his unerring wisdom.'

The Emperor hesitates not one moment. By the close of the day following that upon which the messenger arrives he is on his way back to Rome, proclaiming that Cæsar returns to the helm of the state. That fact alone may check the course of the rebellion, and does so.

If the Emperor will come straight into Palestine from Egypt, bearing the edict and granting it, all will go well. So urge his two best and wisest counsellors, Tryphon and Antinous.

For once the Emperor refuses to listen to this advice. He must be faithful to his faithful Senate. The Senate expects him; the Senate has better and later information than he; by going direct to Palestine he may cross or thwart some wise measure which the Senate has taken, and he must not run the risk of befooling the Senate. Moreover, he has no armed force with which to enter a land that may be in rebellion from north to south, from east to west.

There is reason in the argument as well as

determination, prudence as well as caution, loyalty as well as dignity.

And above all reasons, above all subtleties against the design of going first to Palestine, there is the order of Memnon. The command of Memnon is as clear as it is inevitable. Memnon directs to Rome. Neither Antinous nor Tryphon can answer Memnon.

The course is definite; they must to Rome.

Returning, they arrive at Memphis; they will soon reach Alexandria and embark there.

Some, but not all. All except one.

It is necessary that they shall rest for a day or two at Memphis in order to proceed along the branch of the Nile leading to Alexandria, in vessels of a different class from those in which they have descended from Thebes. The changes imply delay.

To pass the time, Hadrian proposes that he, Tryphon, Antinous, and the selected scholars of his Court shall cross the river and once more visit Heliopolis, in order to see what resemblance the inscription on the wonderful obelisk of Osirtasen bears to the inscriptions found in the palaces of Rameses.

The day is fine and all is propitious for the expedition.

They start on a raft apparently well constructed and manageable, but when they have reached the centre of the stream it proves to the Egyptians who have the charge of it to be too heavily laden.

To return is impossible, and the danger every moment increases.

The raft begins to sink!

The raft is loaded with human freight alone, so that it can only be lightened by one at least of that freight plunging from it into the stream.

Who shall it be that shall save the Emperor of the world from the grave of the waters?

In the solemn emergency Antinous comes forth, clasps the hand of Cæsar, kisses it, and while yet the tears from the eyes of the brave soul rest on it and the warmth of the lips remain upon it, leaps into the stream and is seen no more.

The raft rises slowly, is rowed safely back

to the point of the shore near Memphis from which it started, and Cæsar and his followers tread once more the firm earth.

But Antinous?

Boats manned by hands most familiar with the currents of the river are sent out in every direction to find the friend of friends of Cæsar. Rewards, honours, everything are offered to him, to them, who shall bring the beloved to the Imperial mourner, even though it be a dead Antinous.

All come back empty and desolate. Watches are set on the borders of the river for miles upon miles, at the ports, at the landing-places. By day the river is like a procession, by night it is like a feast of lights. Cæsar himself is everywhere where boat can carry him.

It is a vain search.

Antinous is lost to Cæsar for ever. For ever!

Heartbroken, life-broken, bearing in every look, in every act, funereal gloom, the Emperor of the world, long lingering on his weary way, re-enters Rome.

Henceforth let it be the full care of Hadrian to beatify the immaculate being who laid down his life that he, Cæsar, might be saved from death. For such a service there are no honours too magnificent. Antinous must be numbered with the eternal deities. Statues must be raised to the glorious memory of this immortal mortal. A city must bear the name of Antinous; a youth so pure he might have been a virgin, a virgin vestal and sanctified.

Cæsar lives! Antinous is no more!

CHAPTER XIV.

BETROTHED TO FATE.

WHILE solemn events, tending to great changes and tumults, are occurring in the East ; while rumours of war thicken there and the heart of Israel is crying, 'How long, O Lord, how long?' Simeon and Erine, in company with their father, for now Simeon is the legally adopted son of Leon, travel together on foot, unprotected and even unprovided for, from north to south, from east to west of Juverna. In the extreme north they find a mighty causeway and temple, cut out of the solid rock, in which the Titans of old held their festivals to their divinities.

They row into the splendid caverns, arched and sombre, and sing a song of joy which comes back to them in a hundred echoes. They visit magnificent towers, rising like columns of light from the earth, where white-robed priests chant their orisons to the eternal sun and moon and stars. They go with the priests to the heights of the mountains and help them keep alight the sacred fires that never are extinguished. They pass into the south to discover on the coast a volcano not yet extinct, throwing out, at fitful periods, its fire and its ashes, and forming the centre of a volcanic region in the face of a glorious bay leading into a southern sea of emerald brightness. To the shores of this volcanic bay the winds have wafted from tropical and subtropical lands the seeds of richly-coloured flowering plants, which spring up, luxuriantly, amongst the volcanic débris and yield a weird beauty that can only be appreciated by being directly seen. In the emerald waters Leviathan lies by, a friend and wonder of all the coast and of all who sail past. They go on board the beautiful vessel, and putting up her white sails skim along the coast-line of the south from the centre to the extreme eastern boundary, then to the extreme western and back to the centre. The water is so clear that, when Leviathan is at rest, they can see to the floor of the sea and the varied life that is there. From the land the scent of the flowers diffuses over the sea, and the stars, they think, shine brighter than they ever did before. Their own constellation is there, and Orion and the gentle Pleiads,

> Who seek all night their lost and wandering sister.

Every star in its course blesses them. So do the people, the noble and romantic people. When Leviathan comes to the different landing-places the people put out in their boats and canoes to say 'Welcome!' bringing with them fruits, fresh water, and flowers. They carry with them also their musical instruments, with which they make the heart gladder than with wine, for wine and all its allies is as unknown in the Island of Peace and Beauty, the pure Juverna, as the poisonous reptile which cannot live on the soil. Simeon, who has heard so much in favour of wine in his Eastern life, wonders at seeing so much happiness where wine is not to be found. Leon explains to him that the secret of the existence of the Island of Peace and Beauty lies in the absence of wine. Their sacred scriptures tell them that in the future homes of the blessed, into which they shall pass after death, there is no such evil thing, and quotes to him a verse which, interpreted as near as a foreign tongue will permit, runs :—

> Wine would make glorious heaven a raging hell;
> Make every parched tongue a tongue of fire
> Which water could not quench; make life a dream
> Of falsehood, fury, and debauchery.

Simeon marvels, but Erine who is his prophetess, supports Leon, and a prophetess is beyond argument.

Sometimes Leon and Simeon discuss points of faith and morals, and mysteries the most sublime.

Simeon has been brought up in the strictest form of the Mosaic school. He has no knowledge of any future life, no belief in any future reward or punishment. The God of Moses, according to his view, is the present, ever-avenging, ever-sustaining Omnipotence. His will is to be done on earth. His will is law, which He has revealed through His commandments to His people. Other people have laws, but not His law. Simeon and the chosen have His law, and they have no desire that any other people should have it. One day, no doubt, for the mouth of the Lord hath spoken it, He will, through his chosen ones, establish a kingdom of universal righteousness, a kingdom of glory which shall never pass away; but it will be a kingdom of righteousness and perpetuity, because it will be ruled by and through His laws; and it will be a kingdom of this earth. Men will live as now, die as now; they will pass into the eternal silence as eternal silences; but the kingdom will remain an everlasting kingdom, because it will be under the everlasting commandments, read and kept and interpreted by the elect of the people of the city of Zion, which is to be the city of the elect.

This is what Akiba has taught Simeon, with the addition that he, Simeon, is to be the Messiah who shall re-establish the law and lay the foundations of Zion itself, the new, the holy Jerusalem; the home and house of the God of Jacob, in which His honour shall dwell for evermore.

To the views of Simeon Leon has his answer. He also has his scriptures, which teach him what he feels to be a nobler and higher reading of the supreme and ruling power and mysterious Lord of the heavenly sphere. The views of Simeon he holds to be those of a sect or race exclusive and limited. He cannot admit that the Divinity he recognises can ever specially favour one race or one people. His great divinity gives, he reverently assumes, the reasoning soul to all the children of men, and blesses all who learn and know the laws which govern life and nature.

To know is to live and to love ; not to know is to hate ; to hate is to die.

Listening to the story of Simeon, as he has often heard it, about the release of the Israelites from their Egyptian bondage, Leon suggests respectfully that the Mosaic ordination, which concentrated all law and all reward and all punishment in the immediate will of the Power declared by Moses, was a necessary condition of the liberation ; that it kept the people together ; that it enabled them to establish a peculiar system of government which had its history, and which, without any dispute, had demonstrated that a people could, under peculiar circumstances, be and become a powerful people, on a purely worldly basis, under the guidance of a spirit not of this world but of all worlds, which by the voice of their lawgivers and prophets spoke to them.

'But see,' he adds, 'the result : these very people are now under Roman sway; the Roman divinities have conquered them and rule them with a rod of iron.

The chord of life in Simeon is touched now. It is all true what the wise Leon has said. But the chosen people have broken from him who chose them, they have been punished by him who chose them, and at last, the punishment all but concluded, the time has come when the deliverer is at hand who shall fight the rude enemy, re-establish the everlasting kingdom, and make Zion the centre of all the happiness that shall spring from the law of the omnipotent, omnipresent and invisible Spirit, whom no one can see and live, and whose Holy Name—blessed be it!— can be uttered by no son of his people.

Erine, sweet Erine, art thou listening to this thy fate, for what is Simeon's fate is thine?

Leon, at least, listens, and sighs. If an ordinary man, however great a scholar of his own country, had ventured to talk in such a strain he would have accounted him mad; but this, being sent to him through fire and through water, is not ordinary. He has a destiny, and the destiny is revealed to him, Leon, in directions which no one can gainsay.

The Lion of Judah must play his preordained part, let come what may. In the end it will all be according to the Divine will here or hereafter, for Leon the Wise believes that every man will be according as he has been.

Leviathan is directed to leave the southern coast and skirt the western until she shall be signalled by the sun's rays to meet her chief and his beloved belongings. For themselves they will proceed to the west by land, will diverge towards the centre of the island to see the forest temple of Elbana; will then strike northernward again with a bearing towards the west; will visit a famous city of marble, and after that, going directly west, will rejoin their vessel and make an outward cruise, perhaps to the south-western Cassiterides, or to Ultima Thule, the last place of the northern earth known to them.

They make their journey to the western side of the island on foot, that they may miss nothing of the extreme beauty of lake and wood. Surely such lakes were never elsewhere known. On these lakes the women, in dresses of white and sashes of red, take the oar in turn with their husbands, and sing at the labour as if engaged in a pastime and a pleasure. They know not the name of work. Their husbands join in songs and stories, songs and stories of love and harmony, specially appropriate to the matchless lovers, whom they admire as something more than the ordinary types of human kind.

The songs of the men and the women are rivalled by the songs of the birds. The nightingale sings to them with immortal sweetness. Erine wonders at evetide what manner of bird this can be. The next morning one is brought to her for her particular admiration. She nestles it in her bosom and sings to it so persuasively that when she offers it its liberty it lingers ere it flies away. At night, when their boat is floating under the woods, a bird breaks forth into song above their heads. The sailors say it is the bird that left the breast of Erine, and that it sings her song. Night after night this same event recurs, so that at last the bird that sings the song of Erine the beautiful becomes a tradition lapsing into words and melody :—

The Song of Erine.

Flutter! flutter! heart to heart,
    Maiden's heart so near to mine.
Flutter! flutter! we must part,
    I to my love, thou to thine.
    Trill! trill! trill! in song divine.

Warble! warble! voice to voice,
    Maiden's voice so like to mine.
Warble! warble! we rejoice
    I for my love, thou for thine.
    Trill! trill! trill! in song divine.

Listen! listen! ear to ear,
    Maiden's ear attuned to mine.
Listen! listen! let no tear
    Fall from my love nor from thine.
    Trill! trill! trill! in song divine.

Left to their own devices the lovers would gladly linger in this sweet and exquisite elysium for any length of days, for the wings of love and of time beat synchronously, and one is as the other. But even elysium must have an end, and under the guidance of their father the next chapter of their happy pilgrimage is commenced and carried forth.

They return from the lakes by a northeasterly route along a grand and unique roadsward, through winding avenues of trees leading to Elbana. They pass through lovely villages, in each of which they find a home; for here there are no poor and no rich, no savage luxury, no war, no fury of strife, no wild beast, no serpent, no venomous thing in the whole land.

Pursuing their way by easy stages they enter at length a forest larger than any they traversed in the sister island, in which they pass through pathways of embowering trees straight as the course of an arrow. Arch upon arch of leafy canopy overshadows them within tervening windows of light which open like partitions of the firmament and produce an effect on their minds as if the firmament itself were descending towards them, and as if stars were faintly seen in the light of day.

Along these avenues of light and shade they meet the many who are coming from or going to the grand and central wonder of all this island of the blessed : the scholar who officiates at the altar, clothed in a vestment white as the purest snow ; the poet or prophet, the scholar of the skies, wearing the vestments of his sphere, the ethereal robe of the canopy, with stars that brighten it, and the sun that fills it with his splendour; and others who, like the wise Leon, wear the mantle of the globe, the emerald green that clothes the earth as with a garment, and who gather from the earth the thousand upon thousand of secrets which she holds in trust for those who ask her for her treasures.

Mixed with these are they of simpler mind and manner, who live for themselves in their own little worlds; not selfish, as having no one's welfare save their own in view, but living in modest seclusion, wanting no more than they possess, and content to live and die in the lap of felicity.

They reach at last the temple of temples, the temple of the forest of Elbana, in the heart of glad and smiling Juverna.

From the nearest point on the eastern side of the island a little arm of the silvery sea puts itself forth from the ocean, as if the ocean and the oceans wished to touch the margin of the sacred place.

An open-roofed expanse of green sward is

entered by a winding passage of trees at the westernmost part, a floor of grass four hundred cubits in length, towards the east, and three hundred wide; a vast nave, with columns of massive lofty trees on each side in regular order, the boughs of which arch over to each other, and at small distances let in light which strikes the verdant floor below and fills all the space with the colours of the earth and the sun.

At the extreme eastern end of this temple, separated by a cross line of trees from the rest of the nave, is the central altar, on which burns, as it has burnt for ages, the sacred fire of Elbana in the heart of the island of Juverna.

Reverently and gracefully the three pilgrims approach the sacred fire and cast their offerings of choice cedar wood upon it.

Clothed in pure white robes of ceremony, Simeon and Erine kneel on the sacred stone before the eternal symbol of life and being and power; the power that binds and loosens, destroys and constructs, tears to pieces and brings together, kills and makes alive.

It is the hour of their betrothal, an hour in which love conquers as nothing else can.

Simeon, thou slave of love, how didst thou cast that bundle of cedar wood on the fire of the unholy one, the Baal of thy father's enemies? Fie, Simeon! thou who met a wild beast and became a torch rather than cast a pinch of incense on the altar of Cæsar! Fie, indeed; to let the god of love cajole and command thee, and prove what a slave thou art!

It is the solemn hour of the betrothal of Simeon and Erine; the betrothal of the hope of an oppressed people with the flower of living flowers of the Island of Peace and Beauty; of Juverna, the gem of the western sea.

It is their betrothal according to the ceremonial, ancient and beautiful, of the old and poetical faith in which Leon and all his race believe. It is a ceremonial symbolising, in the simplest and yet most august type, a perpetual existence through the phases of death, of life, of immortality.

The eternal existence is always there in the fire that never ceases to burn.

The two lovers kneeling in its presence are symbols of the spirit kindling but not yet kindled. Into the hand of each is placed a torch shaped as a sheaf of corn, but unlighted.

As they kneel they join their sheaves together by the extreme ends and hold them like an arch over their heads. Then one of the priests of the altar lights another torch from the sacred fire and brings it to Leon, who lights from it the two torches held by the loving pair.

Their combined torches alight, Simeon and Erine rise, and bending their heads carry the flame to the foot of the altar.

They now turn their backs to the sacred fire, and facing the congregation hold still on high the united blazing sign. The priest receives from them the symbol, and raising it over them, as they once more kneel, pronounces the blessing.

Then casting the combined torch into the fire of the altar, and waiting until it is quite consumed, he explains to them the meaning of the ceremonial. That when they first stood before the sacred fire they were individual, separate, ephemeral. Now they have taken the first step towards a new state; the fire has welded them together; they are charged with its living influence, and in time they shall be permitted to represent its immortality; they shall reproduce the fire of life for the ages to come.

And so he bids them depart in peace, preparing for the happier day when the betrothal shall be confirmed and they twain shall be one.

They leave the altar, to traverse sweetly and alone the mazes of this marvellous natural temple: through side isles bedecked with richest flowers in honour of the ceremony in which they have played the chief part; past fountains of water bright as silver streaming from ewers of gold; through glades in which unseen musicians play entrancing melodies; through caverns lighted with what seem to be myriads of fireflies on the branches of trees, like fruits of fire.

At last, wearied with the very richness of delight, they return to the central nave to rejoin the father of their love.

Re-entering by a side aisle they discover Leon in converse with a stranger. The face of Leon is cast down and full, very full, of sorrow.

The stranger with whom he is speaking has his back to them, but Simeon knows at a glance to whom the massive shoulders belong.

The Numidian, with whom he was led to fight in the camp in Siluria! The Numidian, as he turns to them his handsome noble face, looks down with equal sorrow on their eager, anxious, beauteous expression.

He takes from his bosom a scroll written in Hebrew characters and presents it to Simeon.

It is short, decisive, peremptory :—

To SIMEON, THE SON OF A STAR.

Prince of Israel. The time has come when all thy people wait for their deliverer, and when the hour is ripe for their deliverance.

The messenger Eli, the trusted of Huldah the prophetess, the daughter of Elkanah of Cæsarea, bears this scroll and will bring thee to thy place and to thy holy duty.

AKIBA.

Written at Joppa in the tenth month and twelfth day of the year of the great deliverance.

No more, no more, my gentle Erine, no more of that look of terror and despair!

Blind us not, sweetest of maidens; strike us not dead with that look of terror and despair!

His fate has come, and to it thou art as betrothed as to himself.

One long embrace, in which thy conscious soul retreats into thy heart and leaves thy senses void!

Awake! awake! to find thyself once more transferred to thy father's loving arms, still in the mighty temple of the skies, with night drawing near and the curtains of the eternal illuminated with his million fires falling over the windows of the sun.

Let that gentle priest, dear Erine, his own eyes wet with tears, direct thee; and let that strong guardian of thine, thy first, thy truest protector, bear thee to the place of rest.

'Father mine, is he gone?'

'Gone, my own, and now far, far away. But be thou brave and hopeful, for he will return to his betrothed.'

'Yea, father mine; he shall return when the earth burns like that immortal fire! Return as one of the stars that shall ride into the confused mass to find his love. Then, perchance, we may again be one.'

'Nay, my darling, this is wildness of love; he shall return a great ruler and prince, to claim thee again, but neither in clouds nor fire. Thou hast but to be firm and hopeful and trustful, and all shall be bright, aye, brighter than ever.'

A kiss of trust seals the lips of Leon.

'Father, I am thy little child again until he reclaims me.'

And so, father and daughter once more, Leon and Erine Leoline, follow their willing guide, to commence their days, or months, or years of hope, expectation, and faith in him whom they have lost until his mission is fulfilled.

CHAPTER XV.

TO BITHER, THE 'HOUSE OF LIBERTY.'

THE uprising of the Jews in Cyprus and afterwards in Palestine is an event quite as serious as had been represented, through the Senate, to Cæsar. The Romans threw the whole fault upon the Jews, but, in truth, the error was originally entirely Roman. The Roman governor of Cyprus was not without blame. It was his bad fortune and folly to look upon the Jews as an inferior as well as a conquered race, and while he did not scruple to borrow money of them at usury of a ruinous kind, were it duly paid, he constantly forgot to pay any at all, and when complaint was made visited the complainants with condign punishment for presuming to seek their legal if not their honest gains.

In one of these disputes a Jew, who was a freed man of Rome, interposed on behalf of his fellow countrymen, and being a man of position and learning, threatened, through his powerful friend Fortunatus, whom we know, to get the whole particulars sent to Phlegon, the secretary of Hadrian.

The governor, to cut matters short and prevent an exposure, which he very much dreaded, took occasion of Hadrian's absence in Egypt to seize this officious interloper, and on a pretence of treasonable offences to lock him up in prison until Cæsar's return.

The act, altogether a gross usurpation of power, led to a demonstration, firm but perfectly peaceful, on the part of the Jews in favour of the injured man. Their act was again turned to a bad account. Some of them were seized in their own homes and were brought before the governor; some of them were condemned to be scourged, and some of them were sent to the cross. Thereupon the whole Jewish population rose, and proceeding to extremities, retaliated on the Roman people, murdering indiscriminately every man, woman, and child they could lay their hands on, driving the comparatively small garrison of Cyprus into its quarters, and keeping it there at starvation-point until relief came from Sardinia, Joppa, and Rome by the arrival of a sufficient body of Imperial troops to beat down the insurrection.

When the news of these proceedings reached Joppa, and the withdrawal of troops showed the extremity to which the Jews of Cyprus had driven their enemies, the students of the schools were excited to actual tumult. It was with the extremest difficulty that Akiba, who was, fortunately, at that time at Joppa, could hold them from open revolt. From Joppa the contagion spread all over the province, and specially in Jerusalem.

Rufus, quite unequal to meet the emergency, at first vacillated. He was asked what had become of the promised edict. He refused to answer. He was asked if Cæsar were at Rome. He announced, truthfully or untruthfully, that he did not know, and then, changing his tone, said that he declined to tell. He refused a memorial that was sent to him expressing the loyal feelings of the Jewish people, as a deceit and a delusion, and immediately afterwards he promised to send a special courier to Rome to bring back the new ordinances with Cæsar's approval, but he failed so to do.

Finally, under great pressure, he sent for Akiba from Joppa to Jerusalem, and promised him to carry out all the reforms that had been proposed as far as he dare, on his own responsibility, and he commissioned Akiba to go from town to town to bear and confirm the promise.

Akiba was dealing with water. Wherever he went he found the name of Rufus a byword amongst Romans and Jews alike. The officers of the Roman army held Rufus of no account whatever, the Jews despised him; and both agreed on this one point, although on other points they hated each other to the death.

The political complaint of the Jews had become suicidal. The Jews would rather run on the swords of their hated enemies than see those swords hanging over them day by day, without knowing when they would fall.

A more dangerous crisis can never exist anywhere at any time: under it rebellion is inevitable.

The acute mind of Akiba recognised the

position of affairs sharply and logically. The fight must come; the only question was, when?

The Romans were never worse commanded, never in a poorer state of preparation for hostilities. The Jews were never more resolute; could they be armed, and could they have a leader, they were invincible. They have no arms, except a few of an almost hopeless kind, but if they had a leader, a Messiah, who could lead them to even one minor victory he would soon lead them to more, and then arms will quickly be forged, for every scholar knows how to make a sword, a javelin, a bow, a dart, a shield, and something else.

In his journeyings Akiba has with him Elkanah, who is all for action. Though he be crucified again, he is all for action.

A fig for crucifixion! What is crucifixion to a man who has once gone through it, and who sees before him the glory of saving his country from the rule of the tyrant? He, Elkanah, has been saved once. 'Is the arm of the Lord shortened that it cannot save again?'

'To your tents, O Israel!'

They reach Scythopolis. Here the Roman power is concentrated, and Elkanah almost doubts. The behaviour of the Roman officers is insolent even to the renowned Akiba. It is not wise to stay at the place. They will move to the school which has been founded to the north of the Sea of Galilee, to Bither, the 'House of Liberty.'

The decision is not a moment too early. A few more hours, and Akiba with all his suite would be lying in the fortress waiting the will of the Emperor. Injured they would not be, but they would be held for Cæsar. Fortunatus is with the garrison, and he has his own views. He would be pleased to have so grand a scholar in durance and bound friendship near to him waiting for Cæsar.

They escape and reach Bither, an out-of-the-way place, where there is no Roman camp near. It is too small a place, according to Rufus, to be worth putting under guard. It has no fortifications and it requires none, but a little deep Jewish art has turned its natural strength, without display, into great strength, and the school is becoming immense.

The news that Akiba and his friends are

approaching Bither has preceded them. As they enter the place they are met by a procession of scholars, headed by a woman who strikes the cymbals over her head and dances to the sound.

A moment of surprise and recognition, and the dancer, at the feet of Elkanah, is receiving his paternal blessing, while loud acclamations, in which Akiba joins, follow as the lookers-on learn that Huldah, the long-lost daughter of Elkanah and Israel, has been restored to her father and her people.

The recognitions over, they enter the 'House of Liberty' with rejoicings such as have not been heard in all Palestine since the days when the great Solomon was king and the Temple was the pride of the earth.

It is a triumphal procession to the 'House of Liberty.' The daughter of Elkanah, seizing once more her cymbals, leads the way, and with clash of the ringing metals tells in voice of song her escape back to her people.

The Song of Deliverance of Huldah, the Child of Elkanah.

'Huldah, child of Elkanah,
Huldah, child of the chosen,

Sings of her flight from the grave;
Grave in the mother of rivers,
Mother and river of life,
Flowing from lands of the sun,
Feeding the lands of the Pharaohs
With palm trees, olives and grain.

'Huldah, child of Elkanah,
Huldah, child of the chosen,
Obeying the will of Him,
The Mighty One of Israel,
Lived in the courts of the king
Whose power, centred in Rome,
Extends to the ends of earth.
A king who saved her from shame,
Made her a prince of his house,
His comrade by land and sea,
His light in the days of gloom,
His counsellor, guide and friend.

' He, the great king of the earth,
Stood on the footstool of death,
The river of Egypt below
Ready to swallow him up,
As one trampling its glory,
Its rider but not its Lord;
His foot, his feet, in the grave,
Grave of the river of life!

'Huldah, child of Elkanah,
Huldah, child of the chosen,
Casting her life from the scale
Into the mother of rivers;
Saving the Cæsar from death,
Floating away with the stream,

Stream of the river of life,
Reaching a bend of the land,
Kneels on the Sinaite shore,
Asking the God of her race,
God of her Fathers of old,
What she is saved to perform
For the glory of his name.

' Huldah, child of Elkanah,
Huldah, child of the chosen,
Hears from the Heav'n of Heavens;
Hears, like the holy Moses,
Kneeling in self-same place,
The voice, the voice of the Lord
Descending out of the cloud :
The voice, the word of the Lord !

' " Huldah, child of Elkanah,
Huldah, child of the chosen,
Cast off the garments of man,
Put on the garments of white,
Garments of woman's attire,
Hid in the tower of Migdol,
On the highway to the land,
Land of my people, Israel.

' " Huldah, child of Elkanah,
Huldah, child of the chosen,
Go as my spirit shall lead thee,
Go as my hand shall feed thee,
Do as my people shall need thee
Under the word of the Lord."

' Huldah, child of Elkanah,
Huldah, child of the chosen,

TO BITHER, THE 'HOUSE OF LIBERTY' 287

> Treasured the words in her heart,
> Did as the Lord had told her;
> Wandered the wilderness,
> Wandered through hail and wind,
> Wandered through foes of beasts,
> Wandered through foes of men,
> Wandered through Canaan,
> Wandered through Galilee
> To Bither, home of the free.
>
> 'Huldah, child of Elkanah,
> Huldah, child of the chosen,
> Ready to slay or be slain,
> Sings to sound of the cymbals:
> Cæsar is paid by his life,
> Huldah is free for the war;
> Waiting for him who shall come
> Hither to Bither! Messias!
> Hither! The Son of a Star.'

It is difficult to describe the stages of rapt enthusiasm which the congregation that accompanies Huldah express as they make what may be called a triumphal entry into the school of Bither lying to the north of the Sea of Galilee. At each stanza Huldah rests, repeating the stanza if it seems to her not to be understood. Between each stanza, moreover, she clangs the cymbals more vigorously, and the people, led by Elkanah, sing out in rapture the loud and joyous Alleluia. Elkanah is wild with frenzy. Lame no longer, he dances with delight, and a miracle is believed again to have been wrought in him. It is the miracle of exultation after years of oppression.

'Cæsar with all his legions is at our feet. Cæsar falls! The Lord God Omnipotent reigneth! Alleluia! Alleluia!'

Tinnius Rufus never made a greater mistake than when he left the school of Bither a school without a Roman garrison.

The quick eye of Akiba detects, the moment he enters Bither, the admirable way in which all things are bestowed. The schools are fortified and the synagogue itself is a fortification; but arms, weapons of offence and defence, earthworks, forts, and a good tower for observation, are still wanted for warlike purposes, and much is wanted for beauty.

What has been accomplished so far is the work of Huldah, who has been trained in the best military training of the world. Give her the same legions, and she is a match for the great Severus himself.

As it is, she will have to deal with untrained Jews, who have never tasted war. She will have to turn enthusiasm into discipline, one of the hardest of human problems.

She will have another trouble which she duly recognises, and which is ever a solemn trouble in the organisation of revolt for freedom.

In a conquered people there always exists a small number of men who are disinclined to move. A selfish regard for their own comfort or safety actuates this minority. A selfish admiration of successful power, and a hope to have a part in ruling by submission to a superior force, are inducements to remain in amity even with the oppressor. This causes a weakness in the ranks of the rebellious majority; for some one of the failing, unsympathetic band is sure to turn traitor, to reveal plans, to expose dangers, to denounce conspirators.

Akiba has foreseen this danger in regard to Bither of Galilee. Not a man is here who is not sworn and trusty; but he is not so sure of all who are within the bounds of the Roman garrisons in Palestine.

On these and many other points Huldah and Akiba hold what may now fairly be called councils of war in the school of Bither, after the excitement is over. Elkanah drops into his true place. He is an enthusiast who must be kept in control, but he is, nevertheless, shrewd and keen as a bird of prey in his observation. They call him the eagle on the watch-tower.

They are of one mind, that for the present Elkanah and Huldah shall remain secluded at Bither in Galilee. Here an army of students shall be drilled, here the natural fortifications shall be still more improved, and here arrangements for a great city, the new Jerusalem, shall be made ready for the reception and home of the deliverer.

Meantime Akiba himself shall return to Joppa to receive Simeon the deliverer, for whom, as Huldah knows, the faithful Eli has been sent, and who is sure to come.

Simeon shall be brought to Bither, to find an invincible army of Zion; he shall raise in Bither the standard of freedom; he shall be crowned in Bither King of Israel and Judah with all the solemnity of the crowning of Saul.

David and Solomon; he shall march out of Bither from victory to victory; he shall rebuild the Holy Place; and he shall reign in righteousness, a star out of Jacob, a sceptre out of Israel.

Huldah, the child of the chosen, remains in her place. She has passed through the fire of doubt, and remains in her place. To her, unwittingly, Hadrian is paying divine honours, while she for him is forging war to the death. No, not for him, but for his power. Towards him, personally, she feels a friendship time will never extinguish; she pities his afflictions, and she experiences sincerest gratitude for all his kind protection and Imperial favour. But, as the heavenly voice has told her, she, in return, has saved his life at the risk of her own; he is nobly repaid, and now her people are her first care.

This is her invariable argument, firm as a rock, deep rooted, and fixed on something still firmer.

For beneath the outward argument is another from the woman's inner nature, the hope that the one and only love she ever felt from the bottom of her heart, love surpassing that for Elkanah and all the world beside, may one day be requited.

She prays not for the first place in the glory that is sure to come, but after the king shall be proclaimed, and when his throne is secure; when he has brought liberty to Israel and has made conquering peace with Hadrian, shall not she, who has done so much to bring about such splendour of victory, shall not she share the throne with the victor, his queen, his lover, his faithful wife unto death?

Sublimely uplifted by the hope that such shall be her rich reward; filled with bright and holy presages of what she will do when those hopes are realised; seeing in her noble forecast the temple she will help to raise; listening with inspired hearing for the triumphant shouts that shall declare the Temple gates opened for the elect before the living earth was born or the sons of God sought the daughters of men; emboldened to believe that her children and her children's children shall sit on the throne of David; charged with these exalted aspirations, she, Huldah, with more than human self-control, still binds herself first and foremost to the horns of the altar of faith.

Not until every step of final victory has been trodden, every sacrifice made, every sacrifice justified, will Huldah, the child of Elkanah, will Huldah, the child of the chosen, make her desires known to any one save to Him 'who pondereth the heart, keepeth the soul. and rendereth to every one according to the works that are performed in His name and for His kingdom.'

END OF THE SECOND VOLUME.

www.ingramcontent.com/pod-product-compliance
Lightning Source LLC
Chambersburg PA
CBHW032052230426
43672CB00009B/1567